First World War
and Army of Occupation
War Diary
France, Belgium and Germany

4 DIVISION
12 Infantry Brigade,
Brigade Trench Mortar Battery
11 June 1916 - 30 April 1918

WO95/1509/2

The Naval & Military Press Ltd
www.nmarchive.com
Published in association with The National Archives

Published by

The Naval & Military Press Ltd

Unit 10 Ridgewood Industrial Park,

Uckfield, East Sussex,

TN22 5QE England

Tel: +44 (0) 1825 749494

www.naval-military-press.com

www.nmarchive.com

This diary has been reprinted in facsimile from the original. Any imperfections are inevitably reproduced and the quality may fall short of modern type and cartographic standards.

© **Crown Copyright**
Images reproduced by permission of The National Archives, London, England, 2015.

Contents

Document type	Place/Title	Date From	Date To
Heading	WO95/1509/2 4 Divn. 12 Inf. Brigade Brig Trench Mortar Battery 1916 June-1918 April		
Heading	4th Division War Diaries 12th Infantry Bde 4 T.M.B. 1916 June-1917 Dec		
Heading	12th Inf Bde From-Date Of Formation-June 11th 1916 To-July 31st 1916 Volume X		
War Diary	Authie Woods	11/06/1916	12/06/1916
War Diary	Bertrancourt	13/06/1916	04/07/1916
War Diary	Mailly-Maillet	05/07/1916	10/07/1916
War Diary	Bertrancourt	11/07/1916	16/07/1916
War Diary	Mailly Maillet	17/07/1916	20/07/1916
War Diary	Louvencourt	21/07/1916	21/07/1916
War Diary	Autriel	22/07/1916	22/07/1916
War Diary	Meunynck Farm	23/07/1916	27/07/1916
War Diary	A22d Ref Belgium Sheet 28 N W 1/2000	28/07/1916	30/07/1916
War Diary	A22d	31/07/1916	31/07/1916
Heading	12th T.M.B. (12th Brigade) War Diary From Aug 1st 1916 To Aug 31st 1916		
War Diary	Ref Belgium Sheet 28 N W 1/20000 A22d	01/08/1916	03/08/1916
War Diary	Yser Canal C25a	04/08/1916	19/08/1916
War Diary	Poperinghe	20/08/1916	21/08/1916
War Diary	Bedford House	22/08/1916	31/08/1916
Heading	12th T.M.B 12th Brigade Period From Aug 30th 1916 To Oct 31st 1916		
War Diary	Bedford House	30/08/1916	30/08/1916
War Diary	Poperinghe	31/08/1916	16/09/1916
War Diary	Allonville Near Amiens	17/09/1916	26/09/1916
War Diary	La Neuville	27/09/1916	07/10/1916
War Diary	Citadel Camp	08/10/1916	08/10/1916
War Diary	Trones Wood	09/10/1916	09/10/1916
War Diary	T 8 Central	10/10/1916	23/10/1916
War Diary	Trones Wood	24/10/1916	24/10/1916
War Diary	Citadel Camp	25/10/1916	26/10/1916
War Diary	Treux	27/10/1916	28/10/1916
War Diary	Woirel	29/10/1916	31/10/1916
Heading	4th Division 12th Trench Mortar Battery. December 1916		
Heading	War Diary of 12th Trench Mortar Battery. From. 1st December 1916 To 31st December 1916 Volume VII		
War Diary	Morival	01/12/1916	02/12/1916
War Diary	Mericourt L'Abbe'	03/12/1916	03/12/1916
War Diary	Camps 112 And 16	04/12/1916	04/12/1916
War Diary	Camp 16	05/12/1916	05/12/1916
War Diary	Maricourt	06/12/1916	08/12/1916
War Diary	Fregicourt T29b	09/12/1916	18/12/1916
War Diary	Fregicourt	19/12/1916	22/12/1916
War Diary	Camp 16	23/12/1916	27/12/1916
War Diary	Sailly-Laurette	28/12/1916	31/12/1916
Heading	War Diary of 12th Trench Mortar Battery From 11st January 1917 To-31st January 1917		

War Diary	Sailly Laurette	01/01/1917	22/01/1917
War Diary	Bray	23/01/1917	23/01/1917
War Diary	Suzanne	24/01/1917	30/01/1917
War Diary	Curlu Ravine	31/01/1917	31/01/1917
Heading	War Diary of 12th T.M.B. From: 1st February 1917. To: 28th February 1917		
War Diary	Curlu	01/02/1917	03/02/1917
War Diary	Merriere's Wood	04/02/1917	15/02/1917
War Diary	Suzanne	16/02/1917	19/02/1917
War Diary	Camp 117	20/02/1917	20/02/1917
War Diary	Corbie	21/02/1917	28/02/1917
Heading	War Diary of 12th T.M.B. From 1st March 1917 To 31st March 1917		
War Diary	Corbie	01/03/1917	03/03/1917
War Diary	Mortainville	04/03/1917	04/03/1917
War Diary	Beauval	05/03/1917	05/03/1917
War Diary	Remaisnil	06/03/1917	06/03/1917
War Diary	Boufflers	07/03/1917	21/03/1917
War Diary	Orlencourt	22/03/1917	31/03/1917
Heading	War Diary of 12th T.M.B. From 1st April 1917 To 30th April 1917		
War Diary	Orlencourt	01/04/1917	06/04/1917
War Diary	Y Camp	07/04/1917	09/04/1917
War Diary	H22a 8.8	10/04/1917	11/04/1917
War Diary	Fampoux	11/04/1917	11/04/1917
War Diary	H 14a	12/04/1917	13/04/1917
War Diary	G 11	14/03/1917	19/03/1917
War Diary	France St B.N.W.	17/04/1917	17/04/1917
War Diary	G 11	18/04/1917	18/04/1917
War Diary	Montan-Escourt	20/04/1917	20/04/1917
War Diary	Manin	21/04/1917	21/04/1917
War Diary	Beaufort	22/04/1917	22/04/1917
War Diary	Le Cauroy	23/04/1917	26/04/1917
War Diary	Sars-Lez-Bois	27/04/1917	27/04/1917
War Diary	Tilloy-Les-Hermaville	28/04/1917	28/04/1917
War Diary	G.17	29/04/1917	29/04/1917
War Diary	H16b 7.4	30/04/1917	30/04/1917
Heading	War Diary of 12th T.M.B. Period, From 1st. October, 1917. To 31st October, 1917.		
War Diary	D28. C2 B2.1	01/10/1917	01/10/1917
War Diary	B22 B8.5	02/10/1917	07/10/1917
War Diary	S20 U29.93	08/10/1917	13/10/1917
War Diary	S B20 B48	14/10/1917	16/10/1917
War Diary	H.Q At Lt 5.6	17/10/1917	17/10/1917
War Diary	LI D 56	18/10/1917	18/10/1917
War Diary	Montenescourt	19/10/1917	23/10/1917
War Diary	G 27b 9.0	24/10/1917	31/10/1917
Heading	War Diary of 12th T.M.B. Period:- From 1st. November 1917 To 30th November 1917.		
War Diary	Arras	01/11/1917	08/11/1917
War Diary	N5a00.80	08/11/1917	15/11/1917
War Diary	Dale Trench	16/11/1917	17/11/1917
War Diary	Dale Tr	17/11/1917	17/11/1917
War Diary	N5s 00.80	18/11/1917	24/11/1917
War Diary	Arras	24/11/1917	30/11/1917

Heading	War Diary of 12th T.M.B. Period From 1st December 1917 To 31st December 1917		
War Diary	Field	01/12/1917	18/12/1917
War Diary	Arras	19/12/1917	25/12/1917
War Diary	Bde Supply	26/12/1917	31/12/1917
Heading	4th Division 12th T.M.B January To April 1918		
Heading	War Diary of 12th T.M.B. Period From-1st January 1918 To-31st January 1918		
War Diary	Nsd 8.7	01/01/1918	11/01/1918
War Diary	Nsd 80.70	09/01/1917	11/01/1917
War Diary	Anas	12/01/1917	18/01/1917
War Diary	N 8 D 6.7	19/01/1918	31/01/1918
Heading	War Diary of 12th T.M.B. Period From 1st February 1918 To 28th February 1918		
War Diary	N 5 D 8.7	01/02/1918	06/02/1918
War Diary	Berneville	07/02/1918	12/03/1918
War Diary	Arras	13/03/1918	19/03/1918
War Diary	17 B 10-20	20/03/1918	31/03/1918
Heading	12th Brigade 4th Division 12th Light Trench Mortar Battery April 1918		
Heading	War Diary of 12th Trench Mortar Battery Period 1st April 1918 To 30th April 1918		
War Diary	I7B 10-20	01/04/1918	07/04/1918
War Diary	Simoncourt	08/04/1918	11/04/1918
War Diary	Busnes	12/04/1918	12/04/1918
War Diary	L'Ecleme	13/04/1918	27/04/1918
War Diary	W 8 D 85.60	28/04/1918	30/04/1918

WO 95 1509/2

4 DIVN.
12 INF. BRIGADE
BRIG. TRENCH MORTAR BATTERY
1916 JUNE – 1916 APRIL

4th Division
War Diaries
12th Infantry Bde
L.T.M.B.
~~June to October~~
~~1916~~

1916 JUNE — 1917 DEC

Army Form C. 2118.

Vol 4

WAR DIARY
or
INTELLIGENCE SUMMARY
(Erase heading not required.)

Confidential

RECORD OF 12TH T.M. BTTY.
12TH INF BDE

FROM —— DATE OF FORMATION — JUNE 11TH 1916

TO —— JULY 31ST 1916

Volume I

Place	Date	Hour	Summary of Events and Information	Remarks and references to Appendices

Army Form C. 2118.

WAR DIARY
or
INTELLIGENCE SUMMARY
(Erase heading not required.)

Place	Date	Hour	Summary of Events and Information	Remarks and references to Appendices
AUTHIE WOODS	1916 JUNE 11		1/1st & 1/2nd T.M.B's were amalgamated. Church parade. In evening marched to AUTHIE woods near BUS. in buses for night.	
	12		Remained in woods	
BERTRANCOURT	13		Marched to BERTRANCOURT. Battery in billets with 2 UNE of WELLINGTONS.	
	14		Bugging party for trenches. Moved into billets at 4 PM.	

Army Form C. 2118.

WAR DIARY
or
INTELLIGENCE SUMMARY

(Erase heading not required.)

Instructions regarding War Diaries and Intelligence Summaries are contained in F. S. Regs., Part II. and the Staff Manual respectively. Title Pages will be prepared in manuscript.

Place	Date	Hour	Summary of Events and Information	Remarks and references to Appendices
BERTRANCOURT	1916 June 15		Rifle inspection & gas helmet inspection at 11 AM. 2/Lt Brookes & Lt Butler took all available men to Wolf trench to dig. Ammunition reserves. Lt Roberts returned from leave.	
	—16		Men returned from digging at 3AM. Lt Roberts rec'd. orders to take command of the battery with temp'y rank of Capt. Rifle inspection. Men went digging reserve under 2/Lt Matthews.	
	—17		Men returned 3AM. Pte Ball wounded. Inspection of clothing equipment etc. & all deficiencies made up. Digging again in evening under Capt Roberts.	
	—18		Men returned 4AM. All spare kits sent back. Men again went digging in evening.	
	—19		Men finished reserves in evening. 2600 rounds carried up by fatigue party from 11th Bde to reserve from the Quarry. Lt Butler controlled party at Quarry & Capt Roberts saw it into reserve.	
	—20		Men returned at 4AM. In the afternoon party went up under Lt Brooke to clean detonate & cartridge the ammunition. Party returned at 9PM.	
	—21		All available men paraded at 10AM under Lt Whattam to continue with the preparation of ammunition. All officers went up to the line & reconnoitred lines of advance. Working party from Coke H. Wellington July 3 & emplacements for Mortars. Men arrived back at 10 PM.	
	—22		Working party from Brooke returned 3 AM. Rifle inspection 11AM. Men to attend in mess before as intake stoves at 1-3PM. One NCO & 4 men sent up to line with "ammunition carriers". Reported enemy had shelling trench.	
	—23		Heavy thunderstorm; party sent up to clear trench. G.O.C's conference in evening.	
	—24		Artillery bombardment started. [crossed out] Stores blown in by shell. Ammunition in dugouts. Party sent up to see that all was O.K. in eve of thence. No 4 ammunition.	
	—25		Rifle & gas helmet inspection. All mens packs inspected & men kits what should be in packs & what in sandbags. Gas sent over from our lines in evening.	

2449 Wt. W14957/M90 750,000 1/16 J.B.C. & A. Forms/C.2118/12.

WAR DIARY or INTELLIGENCE SUMMARY

Army Form C. 2118.

Place	Date	Hour	Summary of Events and Information	Remarks and references to Appendices
BERTRANCOURT	1916 JUNE 26		Men taken over & lectured on dummy trenches. Capt Roberts & 2L Butler reconnoitring route to assembly trenches & saw that all was correct. Regtl order that enemy were likely to shell villages following day. 2Lt WHATHAM went sick.	
	27		Mess pickets, sandbags, & Officers Valises stored in a barn on ACHEUX road. Men paraded to march off to assembly trenches but stopped by order from Brigade stating that they were not to go up that night. Many Mills village Pack Valises reobtained from store. Regtl order from Brigade to inspect ammunition & cartridge containers to detect defective ammunition. All available men at once sent up. Wire came through that Capt Roberts was to report to AA + QMG at 9.30 A.M. Knotted stout bad ammunition & also that doubt now not cartridges were unreliable. Test to be carried out with 8th next morning. Enemy again shelled village.	
	29		Test carried out with officers from 10th & 11th TMBs at 2.P.M. Trained cartridge unreliable. Results of Test sent to Brigade BROOKS	
	30		Packs & Valises dumped in again. Men inspected in fighting order. Many parades at 5 P.M. under 2Lt BROOKS moved to WOLF Trench (assembly Trench). 2nd Party under 2Lt BUTLER at 5.30 & moved to VALLADE Trench. Guns taken up on a waggon by BDE. Capt ROBERTS went to BHQ to synchronize watches, & then proceeded to VALLADE. Four guns in pits in WOLF Trench.	
	JULY 1		At 6 A.M. section in WOLF trench started to report to on the Quadrilateral. After reporting they stood to until 7.20 A.M. when they opened rapid fire which was kept up until 7.30 A.M. firing about 700 rounds. They then allowed their guns to cool, cleaned them & remounted ready to advance. At 9.25 A.M. this section got out of WOLF Trench 2Lt BROWN in charge. As soon as they got out into the open, in rear of the KINGS OWN, they came under very heavy M.G. & rifle fire. They advanced as far as the second German line & at this position two guns were mounted & got into action on to a communication trench, where it was thought the Germans were getting their supply of bombs down.	CHN

WAR DIARY or INTELLIGENCE SUMMARY

Army Form C. 2118.

Place	Date	Hour	Summary of Events and Information	Remarks and references to Appendices
BERTRANCOURT	1916 July 1		After firing several rounds they were bombed out. One gun could not be got away and two jams up by one of our own shells. Two other guns were mounted & got into action further back but had not time to fire before order was given to retire. During the retirement they came under heavy M.G. fire & shower of bombs & whole of this section except 8 men were either killed or wounded. The guns were never got into action again but the few remaining men helped greatly in holding the Germans off with bombs. The Second section left VALLADE at 9.55 A.M. under Capt ROBERTS & Lt BUTLER. Before reaching our own front line 10 casualties had occurred during to M.G. fire. Had to halt there as LANCS FUS. were held up in front. Advancing again we came under heavy artillery barrage. The section found it impossible to advance, a great many casualties occurring before many yards were covered. O.C. remained with this section until 10.45 A.M. & then advanced to German Bde line & tried to get in touch with the Germans First Section but could not do so; owing to missing the units of the Division. O.C. remained there until 6.30 PM when C.O. BEAUFORT HS told me to go back for reinforcements & bombs. On arriving at Bde HQ, reported & received orders to move the few men who had returned to my trenches back into HERBERTS VIEW TRENCH. Mustering in VIEW TRENCH at 2 A.M. we found 1 officer (CAPT ROBERTS) 1 N.C.O. & 18 other ranks with 1 Vickers plate & 2 T.M's. Later on N.C.O. and 5 other ranks reported themselves. Enemy shelled batteries in our rear, several shells dropping short one destroying shell dropping in our trench.	

Army Form C. 2118.

WAR DIARY or INTELLIGENCE SUMMARY
(Erase heading not required.)

Instructions regarding War Diaries and Intelligence Summaries are contained in F.S. Regs., Part II. and the Staff Manual respectively. Title Pages will be prepared in manuscript.

Place	Date	Hour	Summary of Events and Information	Remarks and references to Appendices
BERTRANCOURT	1916 July 3		Enemy shelled batteries again, several hitting French. G.O.C. 6 Cottonwood. Men were employed in bring ammunition back from WOLF Trench, which had been badly harried about, up to PALLADE	
	4	2 A.M.	One gun mounted near LYCEUM. Men again employed recovering ammunition. Recd orders in evening to withdraw guns & billet in MAILLY-MAILLET.	
MAILLY-MAILLET	5		Party sent up to trenches to recover more ammunition, returning about 6 P.M.	
	6		Party sent to BERTRANCOURT to draw sandbacks etc. O.C. went into trenches to choose 4 gun positions near the REDAN.	
	7		Four guns from 10th Bde with gunteams & officers lent to us. Work commenced on emplacements at positions found the previous day.	
	8		Work continued	
	9		Four guns of 10th Bde occupied positions, & registered. Ready to support L.F.6 in a raid to take place early next morning.	
	10		Raid took place but being a failure guns did not fire & were withdrawn to MAILLY-MAILLET. Moved to BERTRANCOURT, being relieved by 11th Bde	

WAR DIARY or INTELLIGENCE SUMMARY

Army Form C. 2118.

Place	Date	Hour	Summary of Events and Information	Remarks and references to Appendices
BERTRANCOURT	1916 July 11		All mens kits etc inspected & deficiencies made up as far as possible	
	—12		Drill — Rifle & Gas Helmet inspection. Received orders that on following day four officers and 36 O.R.'s coming to Battery.	
	—13		Reinforcements arrived. Training commenced. Elements of gundrill & detail of gun	
	—14		Training continued. Gun drill — detail of gun & shell.	
	—15		Training continued. Orders received to shift to Brigade Bombing demonstration on the 17th inst. Arranged details with O.C HRD B.L. Bombing Officer.	
	—16		Rained heavily. Reinforcements continued training on LOUVENCOURT road. Training area. Transport men practised demonstration at BEAUSSART	
MAILLY-MAILLET	—17		Demonstration given at BEAUSSART at 2 P.M. Commander of Battery doing operations. Two guns were used. A preliminary barrage was effected in conjunction with rifle grenade bombers a creeping & barrage lifted, being kept 50 yds in front. Lt General HUNTER-WESTON and 8th Corps were present. At 6.15 P.M. we relieved the 10th T.M.B. in bivouacs near MAILLY-MAILLET. Party of 7 men and 1 N.C.O. went into line to take over emplacements & dugouts	
	—18		Rained heavily. Rifle & Gas Helmets inspected. The M.M.T.S.O. went up to line & reported all correct.	
	—19		Ammunition from BEAUSSART carried to the bivouac. Broke read from Staff Officer in respect ammunition at WHITE CITY & return damaged shells. Lt AVERY sent up into line.	

Army Form C. 2118.

WAR DIARY
or
INTELLIGENCE SUMMARY
(Erase heading not required.)

Instructions regarding War Diaries and Intelligence Summaries are contained in F. S. Regs., Part II. and the Staff Manual respectively. Title Pages will be prepared in manuscript.

Place	Date	Hour	Summary of Events and Information	Remarks and references to Appendices
MAILLY MAILLET	1916 July 20		Ammunition at WHITE CITY inspected. Cartridges & detonators removed from damaged shells. Two men accidentally wounded whilst removing cartridges. Orders read that we should be relieved by 12th Divn on 21st. 6 new guns arrived.	
LOUVENCOURT	21		Relieved by 12th Divn. Marched to LOUVENCOURT where we were billeted for the night	
AUTHEUIL	22		Marched off in rear of KINGS OWN & marched to AUTHEUIL. No 1 Section moved to DOULLENS at 10 P.M.	
MEURYNCK FARM	23		No 1 Section entrained at 2 AM in 2nd train of brigade to CASSEL. No 2 Section followed at 8 AM & entrained at 4.30 AM. Marched independently to MEURYNCK FARM near HOUTKERQUE.	
	24		Gun drill & Squad drill	
	25		Usual parades	
	26		Usual parades. Battery paid out	
	27		Usual parades	
A 22 d Ref BELGIUM Sheet 28 NW 1/20000	28		Marched to HOUTKERQUE & thence with Bde HQ to POPERINGHE. Billets in Camp A22d	
	29		G.O.C.'s Conference. 2Lt MATSON & A/tery reconnoitred Divnl. Reserve line. Usual parades	
	30		Lt A/tery reported at 2nd Army T.M. School. O.C. went with 2Lt MAURDER & Lt IRWIN to reconnoitre (?Trexles) Divisional reserve line. Parades as usual	OAN

2449 Wt. W14957/M90 750,000 1/16 J.B.C. & A. Forms/C.2118/12.

Army Form C. 2118.

WAR DIARY
or
INTELLIGENCE SUMMARY

(Erase heading not required.)

Instructions regarding War Diaries and Intelligence Summaries are contained in F. S. Regs., Part II. and the Staff Manual respectively. Title Pages will be prepared in manuscript.

Place	Date	Hour	Summary of Events and Information	Remarks and references to Appendices
A 22.d	1916 July 31		Parade, as usual.	

2449 Wt. W14957/Mgo 750,000 1/16 J.B.C. & A. Forms/C.2118/12.

Army Form C. 2118.

WAR DIARY
or
INTELLIGENCE SUMMARY
(Erase heading not required.)

Vol II

12th T.M.B. (12th BRIGADE)

WAR DIARY

FROM AUG 1ST 1916
TO AUG 31ST 1916

WAR DIARY or INTELLIGENCE SUMMARY

Army Form C. 2118.

Place	Date	Hour	Summary of Events and Information	Remarks and references to Appendices
Ref BELGIUM 1916 sheet 28 NW 1/20000 A 22 d	Aug 1		Battery in Huts. Brigade in Divisional Reserve	
	-2		Battery paid out	
	-3		Orders recd to relieve 10th TMB on the 4th Aug. Time of march 7.30 PM Trench relief Table recd.	
YSER CANAL C25a	-4		Relieved 10th TMB. 5 guns in line remainder in reserve. Positions of guns 4 in Trench S18a (Near ALGERIAN COT) under 2/Ls MAUNDERS and IRWIN 1 in Trench B13 S18a guns command SOMEUT at MORTALJE EST. B13 gun to barrage ADMIRALS ROAD & command CAVAN TRENCH	
	-5		30 rounds shell sent up to B13. Ammunition sorted out, cleaned + fused.	

WAR DIARY or INTELLIGENCE SUMMARY

Army Form C. 2118.

Place	Date	Hour	Summary of Events and Information	Remarks and references to Appendices
YSER CANAL C25a	1916 Aug 6		L/C L.H. AVERY & Cpl. PICKLES returned from 2nd ARMY T.M. School. 24 rounds shell sent up to S13a.	
		7	2/Lt MAUNDERS left for 4th Divisional School of Instruction. Also Cpl Senior. Pte CLISSOLD ——— 2nd Army T.M. School	
		8	No 2 Section paid out. No 2 Section started out to relieve No 1 at 10.15 in three parties. At 10.30 Gas alarm was sounded & heavy shelling of CANAL, support trenches and communications. First party under Cpl Sibley, proceeding to the detached post, started on red rocket at 10.45 & hurried on. At BOUT.ROAD machine gun fire was so hot that they had to take cover in a ditch until 12 & then proceeded with relief. Second party, Nos 5 & 7 detachments under 2/Lt MATSON, hurried on to H.Q. Lane trenches; stayed there until 12.15; then carried on. Third party, Nos 8 & R detachments under 2/Lt AVERY were shelled immediately after crossing the canal & took cover until 12.30 before proceeding. Relief was complete at 3.30; No casualties in Battery.	

WAR DIARY
or
INTELLIGENCE SUMMARY

Army Form C. 2118.

Place	Date	Hour	Summary of Events and Information	Remarks and references to Appendices
YSER CANAL C 25a	1916 Aug 9		No 2 Section received orders to register next morning & also to commence a new emplacement off SHROPSHIRE Trench NE of TURCO FARM.	
	—10		Registered on MORTALJA EST. at 10 AM. Expenditure 4 rounds. New emplacement chosen. Trench repairs carried out during night. Cleared thorn in screen of trench on left of S18a.	
	—11		Started new emplacement. Trench bombs fired in S18a. 30 rounds Ammunition returned as unserviceable.	
	—12		Ammunition in reserve at WILLOWS cleaned & counted. 6 army whiz bangs now registering the road. No 1 Section relieved No 2. Relief complete at 12 M.N.	
	—13		Pte Chisholm returned from 2nd ARMY T.M. School. 2Lt MATSON left for 2nd ARMY T.M. School. 150 Rifle & gas helmet inspection. 3–4 NCOs class under 2Lt AVERY	
	—14		Wind S.W. Weather very fine. Party of 6 men on new emplacement from 11 PM to 2 Note re Gas recd — No man who has been in a gas cloud should enter a dugout for 24 hours. Any working party should be relieved. 11'O Rifle inspection.	
	—15		Wind S. Cloudy – Slight thunders. Relief changed from 16th to 17th per Brigade order. 11 men on Emplacement. Note on Flammenwerfer – Best defense is to shoot down operators. 11'O Rifle inspection 3—4 NCos class	

2449 Wt. W14957/M90 750,000 1/16 J.B.C. & A. Forms/C.2118/12.

Army Form C. 2118.

WAR DIARY or INTELLIGENCE SUMMARY

(Erase heading not required.)

Place	Date	Hour	Summary of Events and Information	Remarks and references to Appendices
YPRES CANAL C25a	1916 Aug 16	6 PM	Wind SW Cloudy. Party of 6 on emplacement.	
	—17	3 PM	Rain. Gas alarm 3 AM on right. Captured Broke shake Stalks left this front for Russia. Gas cylinders all round salient. Bombing & M.G. activity last night. Relieved No1 Section. Relief complete 10:30. Enemy shelled attack ?gauntope at 6 PM without success. Very quiet night.	
	—18			
	—19		Wind S (changeable) weather showery. Sniped enemy MG positions with rifles & Lewis gun. Relieved at 3 AM by 115 TMB.	
POPERINGHE	—20		Left Canal Bank at 4 AM for POPERINGHE. Rec'd orders to relieve Canadians. scattered fire.	
	—21		O.C. inspected new positions. scattered fire.	
	—22		4 detachments 2 from each section trained from POPERINGHE to YPRES & took over from 8th CANADA TMB. Reinf. from No1 in lieu on R. Scott's teams from No2 with detachment in reserve at Bols HQ. Relief complete at 2 AM 23rd. scattered fire wind E.	
BEDFORD HOUSE	—23		Remainder of Battery arrived at 11:15 PM. Relief complete by 3 AM 24th. Amma. exp'd 18 rounds. scattered fire. Slight showers at 8 PM. Wind E	
	—24		Order rec'd re sanitation from Bn wing. Contents — Latrines. Cookhouse. Lice. Tents. Feet. Enemy shelled tram Slight showers. Wind changeable. Gas alert 9 AM — 4 PM and 9 PM — 12 MN. 40 rounds fired in retaliation for mentle TM's + rifle grenades. 11 AM Pope inspection. Tent & Bn Brush inspection. 230 NCOs class under R. Avery.	OK/? ?

2449 Wt. W14957/M90 750,000 1/16 J.B.C. & A. Forms/C.2118/12.

WAR DIARY or INTELLIGENCE SUMMARY

Army Form C. 2118.

Place	Date	Hour	Summary of Events and Information	Remarks and references to Appendices
BEDFORD HOUSE	1916 Aug 25		Weather fine. Wind strong W. Note from G.O.C. emphasising importance of retaliation on scale of 1/2 shells per rifle grenade upwards. One copy issued to every gunteam. O.C. inspected guns in line at 1 P.M. Pte Maltman excused from 2½ hrs drill rifle & helmet inspection under charge of sergeants (on active service). 1200 Rifle & helmet inspection. 2-3 NCOs class under Lt AVERY. 3-4 NCOs Gobund men on gun.	
	—26		Same parades as yesterday	
	—27		2 gun teams from No 2 section relieved guns in R.H. Sectory. 107 rounds fired in retaliation for jam (?am) + T.M. shells; a dugout was observed hit. 2 rounds fired by No 3 gun at 12 MN. Order received from Brigade to send in a return showing no of rounds fired & reason for firing — results observed.	
	—28		2. Lt IRWIN left for 2nd Army T.M. School. No 1 gun relaid & sighting tripods fixed up. Right guns registered from line near sap hint. Front reconnoitred for suitable O.P's. Requested not to fire after 6 P.M. by G.O. LANCS. FUS. as relief was taking place.	
	—29		No 1 gun registered on support trench at 31 in 48 shots. All guns fired 2 rounds at 6 O'CK stand down. 3-4 P.M. 30 rounds tpy gun fired at front line & supports by Brind. orders. Enemy attempts to evacuate front line. 1 dugout blown up. Enemy retaliated with TM's & shells of all sizes. No casualties. KING ST badly knocked about. 9.30 Bombardment by 18 prs & ans. False alarm of gas at 11.30.	
	—30		An Australian officer (2 A.T.M.B.) + 10 O.R. arrived to reconnoitre position.	

Army Form C. 2118.

WAR DIARY
or
INTELLIGENCE SUMMARY
(Erase heading not required.)

Instructions regarding War Diaries and Intelligence Summaries are contained in F. S. Regs., Part II. and the Staff Manual respectively. Title Pages will be prepared in manuscript.

Place	Date	Hour	Summary of Events and Information	Remarks and references to Appendices
BEDFORD HOUSE	1916 Aug 30		Fired 2 rounds per gun at 5 AM. 5 rounds fired in retaliation for TMs & rifle grenades	
		11 PM	Remainder of relief arrived – relief complete 1 AM 31st inst.	
	-31		Entrained at YPRES for POPERINGHE arriving aming 5 AM – No parades – Rest orders from Bde to Maur. 4 officers & 16 O.R. commencing Sept 2nd	

2449 Wt. W14957/M90 750,000 1/16 J.B.C. & A. Forms/C.2118/12.

Army Form C. 2118.

WAR DIARY
or
INTELLIGENCE SUMMARY

(Erase heading not required.)

12th T.M.B
12th BRIGADE.

PERIOD FROM Aug 30th 1916
TO Oct 31st 1916

Vol I. II. III
4 & 5

Army Form C. 2118.

WAR DIARY
or
INTELLIGENCE SUMMARY
(Erase heading not required.)

Instructions regarding War Diaries and Intelligence Summaries are contained in F.S. Regs., Part II. and the Staff Manual respectively. Title Pages will be prepared in manuscript.

Place	Date	Hour	Summary of Events and Information	Remarks and references to Appendices
BEDFORD HOUSE	1916 Aug 30		Manual 2 rounds for gun at 5 AM. 3 rounds fired in retaliation for T.M's + rifle grenades. 11 PM Remainder of relief arrived — relief complete 1 AM 31st inst.	
POPERINGHE	—31		Entrained at YPRES for POPERINGHE arriving 5 AM — No parades — Recd orders from Brigade to train 4 officers & 16 other ranks, commencing Sept 2nd	
	SEPT 1		Gun drill — inspection of kit, clothing + guns. Stand of No. 7 gun sent to Armourer for repair. 2/Lt MAINDER + Cpl VSerrier returned from 2 ind. School of Instruction.	
	—2		Training class started — Battery on manual parades from 7 AM — 4 PM — 5 PM Battery paid out.	
	—3		9.30 Broke aeroplane overhead — Enemy started shelling town with 8.2's (?) 2/Lt IRWIN back from 2nd Army T.M. School	
	—4		Weather dull. 2/Lt Sn. 2/Lt MAINDER left for 2nd Army T.M. School. Class Gundrill + lectures. 2/Lt IRWIN + 2 O.R. attached Kings own for digging.	
	—5		Weather rainy. Instr. W. Class as above.	
	—6		Weather fine. Instr. W. Parades for class as usual	
	—7		Weather fine. Class continues	
	—8		Weather fine. Instr. N.E. Goualet. Class fired 15 rounds on ranges off CROMBEKE road. Instr. Course of training from trenches	OK Newton

Army Form C. 2118.

WAR DIARY
or
INTELLIGENCE SUMMARY
(Erase heading not required.)

Place	Date	Hour	Summary of Events and Information	Remarks and references to Appendices
POPERINGHE	1916 SEPT 9		Wind E. Weather fine. Class fired 18 rounds. Captain inspected mens kit & clothing.	
	-10		Wind N. Weather fine. Class fired 15 rounds. Recd. defence scheme from Bde. 2/Lt MATSON left for 2nd Army School. 2/Lt MANDER and 40 O.R's returned from 2nd Army T.M. School	
	-11		Cpl SENIOR left for 2nd Army T.M School. Wind N. weather cloudy	
	-12		Wind N. Rain. Class examined. 4 men retained, remainder returned to Butts. 9 men from resting Battalion for instruction	
	-13		Wind — Weather showery. New class started. Parades — 7 — 7.30 A.M. P.T. 10 — 11 — 9-10 Rifle Exercises 10 — 12 — Lecture on Gun Box & Ammo. Carrier 2 — 3 P.M. Gun drill 3 — 4 — Gas helmet drill	
	-14		Parades for class similar to above	
	-15		Ditto. Recd. new type box respirator (small) for Battery.	
	-16		Orders recd. to move from POPERINGHE. Corps Commander inspected Brigade. Left billets at 11 P.M & entrained Battery at HOUDVITRE by 12 P.M. (Class returned to Battalion)	[signature]

Army Form C. 2118.

WAR DIARY
or
INTELLIGENCE SUMMARY

(Erase heading not required.)

Instructions regarding War Diaries and Intelligence Summaries are contained in F. S. Regs., Part II. and the Staff Manual respectively. Title Pages will be prepared in manuscript.

Place	Date	Hour	Summary of Events and Information	Remarks and references to Appendices
ALLONVILLE near AMIENS	1916 SEPT 17	12 AM	Detrained at SALEUX. Marched through AMIENS to POULAINVILLE, leaving 1st & 2nd Lieut 25 O.R. for detraining transport at SALEUX. POULAINVILLE found full of French troops, & had to billet in visible area at ALLONVILLE.	
	-18		2 Lt MATSON returned from 2nd Army Central School. Rained all day. Incidents inconvenience caused by lack of transport for obtaining rations.	
	-19		Parades. Gun drill — Attack practice. Weather showery.	
	-20		Inspected by G.O.C. 4th Divn. at 12.15 AM. Gun drill in afternoon. Weather showery.	
	-21		Gun drill & Attack practice in morning. Afternoon — Squad drill — Gas lecture by Divnl Gas Officer. Tested all new "Small box respirators" in "lachrymatory gas". Weather fine. Parades as usual. Orders recd. re Reporting Casualties.	
	-22		Weather fine. Parades as usual. Adjutants conference at Bde to discuss Reporting Casualties.	
	-23		Weather fine.	
	-24		No parades. Weather fine. Notes on attack experience obtained in SOMME.	
	-25		Weather fine. Orders recd. to remove all kit in lorry at 2 PM. Brigade moves to ALLONVILLE. Orders recd to prepare for Brigade to be now on pack in attack. Orders recd to move on 26th to LA NEUVILLE at 9.16 AM.	
	-26		Weather hot. Arrived LA NEUVILLE at 11.30 AM. Good billets.	

Army Form C. 2118.

WAR DIARY
or
INTELLIGENCE SUMMARY

(Erase heading not required.)

Instructions regarding War Diaries and Intelligence Summaries are contained in F. S. Regs., Part II. and the Staff Manual respectively. Title Pages will be prepared in manuscript.

Place	Date	Hour	Summary of Events and Information	Remarks and references to Appendices
LA NEUVILLE	1916 SEP 27		Fine. Parade 7-7.30 PT 8.45-12.30 gun drill, squad drill, digging in 2.15-4.15 musketry	bayonet fighting
	— 28		Fine. Parade as usual.	
	— 29		Fine. Parade as usual. Red from Bde German description of recent our attacks at La Boiselle in April 1916.	
	— 30		Fine. Parade as usual. Notified that Division would attack LE TRANSLOY.	
	OCT 1		Showery. Digging Emplacements — Night Operations.	
	— 2		Rain. Lecture. Bomb throwing. Played Signallers at football in afternoon. Won 2-1.	
	— 3		Rain. Trench digging practice.	
	— 4		O.C. attended Brigade Operations. 10th & 11th Bde made practice attack on FRAMVILLERS	
	— 5		Weather fine. Battery digging in morning, bathing in afternoon.	
	— 6		12th Bde Operations (Attack on village practised.) Battery paid out. 2/Lt MATSON sent to hospital.	
	— 7		2/Lt AVERY & Sgt BROCKHILL left for 4th Divisional School. Recd orders to move on 8th inst. Recd 8 handcarts from B.A.D.O.S.	
CITADEL CAMP	— 8		Moved from LA NEUVILLE to CITADEL CAMP. Marched with Bde HQ: part of way over appalling cross country tracks, handcarts went all the way by road. Guns taken by motor lorries.	
TRÔNES WOOD	— 9		Moved to TRÔNES WOOD to relieve 167th TMB taking rations on two hand carts. Rest of carts taken to transport lines by section. 3 men left to bring guns up in limbers that evening. Reported to BHQ relief completed by 4 P.M. & recd orders to move next morning to TB central.	

2449 Wt. W14957/M90 750,000 1/16 J.B.C. & A. Forms/C.2118/12.

WAR DIARY
or
INTELLIGENCE SUMMARY
(Erase heading not required.)

Army Form C. 2118.

Place	Date	Hour	Summary of Events and Information	Remarks and references to Appendices
T 8 Central	1916 OCT 10		Moved to T 8 Central. No accommodation. French evacuated. Commenced building dug outs. Officers dug up to accommodate the ground.	
	— 11		Recd orders at 1.30 AM from BHQ to assist artillery in carrying out a Chinese attack. 24 MAUNDERS sent up with 2 guns to fire on enemy trenches. Found impossible to find ammunition taken over, all of which was damp + rusty. G.O.C.s conference — instructions for attack on following day. 2 guns sent up to reinforce with 300 rounds ammunition. No 2 section occupied JOHN BULL trench with 2.6" rounds per gun.	
	— 12		5 AM — 2 guns sent back to TRONES WOOD. Manage recd from 2/LT MAUNDERS to officer that he was shaken + required another officer to help him. Sent back to say he would be relieved same night. Later relief arrived, reported that 2/LT MAUNDERS had left men without instructions + gone sick 2/LT MATSON reported from hospital infantry attacked without success.	
	— 13		Quiet day. Ammunition carried up to time	
	— 14		— ditto —	
			A few rounds fired	
	— 15		Recd orders to assist K.O.Y.L.I in a bombing raid. CAPT. ROBERTS went up to trenches to make arrangements. 87 rounds fired. Raid held up by enfilade fire from M.G.'s one of which was silenced + fired to a few rounds rapid with effect.	
	— 16		2/LT MATSON took No 2 Section up to relieve No 1. All men carried two trench bottles. (Bde order) Report sent in re bombing raid. T8 Central shelled with gas shells at 11.30 PM.	
	— 17		T8 Cent shelled at 4 AM Recd orders at BHQ for operations next morning day. Albeit orders + received line. Ammunition sent up, 50 assault in carrying parties. Guns registered. Attack started at 3.40. At ZERO two guns opened on our party SPECTRUM helping Boche, + one gun on SUNKEN ROAD. At 0+2 all guns fired on SUNKEN ROAD until 0+3. Very heavy shelling recd. 2 hours gas shelling on T8 central also later on, HE + shrapnel. More ammunition sent up in the evening One gun required fire on SPECTRUM. One gun knocked out by HE.	

2449 Wt. W14957/M90 750,000 1/16 J.B.C. & A. Forms/C.2118/12.

WAR DIARY
or
INTELLIGENCE SUMMARY
(Erase heading not required.)

Army Form C. 2118.

Place	Date	Hour	Summary of Events and Information	Remarks and references to Appendices
T8 Central	1916 OCT 19		One gun turret early in morning & returned with gunners whilst being dug out. Fresh gun received. R&L orders that Bole would extend its line to its right; this gun to be left in WINDY trench to defend the left flank & two guns in BURNABY trench by night of 20/21. Rained all day. Found impossible to post guns in BURNABY owing to the state of the trenches; all four left in WINDY.	
	-20			
	-21		Section in JOHN BULL heavily shelled during the morning. Four guns knocked. 7 casualties. WINDY trench also shelled; all guns being hard - one lost, one badly damaged. Fire received. R&T warning orders from BHQ for next attack. Commenced getting guns into position & sent up ammunition	
	-22		Gun position ready. Operation orders recd: viz two guns to be lent to trenches. 2nd MATSON took them up. Ammunition carried up.	
	-23		Orders recd. that Bole would be relieved on night of 23/24. Guns taken in WINDY. 2nd MATSON's section installed in ZENITH trench. Section in WINDY put out of action before ZERO. ZENITH section opened fire from O to O+2 on SUNKEN ROAD	
TRONES WOOD	-24		Officer from 98th & TMB arrived to arrange relief. Guns withdrawn & housed in TRONES WOOD. Relief complete at 10PM.	
CITADEL CAMP	-25		Left TRONES WOOD for CITADEL CAMP	
	-26		Stayed at CITADEL. Kit cleaned. G.O.C. & Divn held conference at BHQ. Movement orders recd	
TREUX	-27		Left at 3.30PM marched to billets at TREUX	
	-28		Kit inspection etc. Movement orders recd.	

WAR DIARY
INTELLIGENCE SUMMARY

Army Form C. 2118.

Place	Date	Hour	Summary of Events and Information	Remarks and references to Appendices
MOIREL	1916 OCT 29		Marched to MERICOURT & entrained at 2 PM for ARAINES	
	—30		Detrained at 12.15 M.M. 29/30 & marched to MOIREL. Battalion in billets at 11.30 AM. Peened all day	
	—31		C.O. sent in report on recent operations	
	Nov 1			Visit by G.O.C.

4th DIVISION.

12th TRENCH MORTAR BATTERY.

DECEMBER 1916.

SECRET

WAR DIARY

OF

12TH TRENCH MORTAR BATTERY.

From: 1st December 1916.
To: 31st December 1916.

Volume VII.

31st Dec. 1916.   F.W. Roberts Capt.
                              Commanding
                         12th Trench Mortar Battery

WAR DIARY or INTELLIGENCE SUMMARY

Army Form C. 2118.

(Erase heading not required.)

Place	Date	Hour	Summary of Events and Information	Remarks and references to Appendices
MORLVAL	1916 Dec 1		Parades as usual. Baths for Battery.	
	- 2		Equipment of Battery with clothing & repair kit completed.	
MERICOURT -L'ABBE	- 3		Battery Paraded at 7AM and marched to DISGMONT. Entrained at 4 PM reaching MERICOURT-L'ABBE at 11 PM. After a hot meal at E.F. Canteen march was continued to Camp 112 (F29 d)	
CAMPS 112 and 16	- 4		which was reached at 5AM. After a short rest march was resumed at 10.35 AM to Camp 16. This camp was reached at 12 noon. (F.30 d.)	
CAMP 16	- 5		Lt MATSON reconnoitred neighbourhood of CORBIES to find accommodation for men & was unsuccessful.	
MARICOURT	- 6		Battery marched at 10.30 AM to camp in neighbourhood of MARICOURT	
	- 7		OC failed to find billets for battery in MARICOURT or CARNOY, so remained at MARICOURT. Both refused Bivouac French on line.	
	- 8		MARICOURT	
FREICOURT Tp 6	- 9		Battery marched to FREICOURT and found accommodation for all in some covered in dugouts August, T.29.b.	

WAR DIARY
or
INTELLIGENCE SUMMARY

(Erase heading not required.)

Army Form C. 2118.

MAP REF. ALBERT 57D.NE.

Place	Date	Hour	Summary of Events and Information	Remarks and references to Appendices
FREGICOURT F.29.b.	Dec. 10		2L IRWIN reconnoitred lines for Gun positions.	WI.
	11		OC reconnoitred line. Owing to state of ground G.O.C. decided not to attempt to get any guns in the line. Battery was ordered to supply working parties to 5th Royston Field Coy.	WI.
	12		All available men employed on carrying trench boards, improving Btts. H.Qrs and R.A.H.Q. dugouts. Pte FAWCETT died before near Bde. H.Q.	WI.
	13		Capt. F.D. ROBERTS returned from leave. Work continued under R.E.	WI.
	14		Working parties - laying of trench boards before line continued.	WI.
	15		Working parties on naval. COMBLES — FREGICOURT road shelled during day. Afternoon enemy aircraft battery position heavily shelled.	WI.
	16		Working parties continued.	WI.
	17		Working parties. Sgt. BROCK HILL wounded at R.E. DUMP.	WI.
	18		Working under R.E. continued. Message recd from DIVISION that arrangements would be made for Xmas to be celebrated on 7th JANUARY.	WI.

WAR DIARY or INTELLIGENCE SUMMARY

Army Form C. 2118.

Place	Date 1916	Hour	Summary of Events and Information	Remarks and references to Appendices
FRÉGICOURT	Dec 19		Work under R.E. cont'd. Four new guns ~~arrived to replace~~ removed from DADOS. Weather very foggy. Lt Irving selected site for gun pits.	All.
	20		Lt Avery with one section carried up material for gun pits. Sent commenced work on it. Working parties were found for R.E. as usual. Casualties - one man wounded.	All.
	21		Work under R.E. cont'd. A small party continued work on gun pits. During the day battery dug out FRÉGICOURT dressing station shelter. Casualties - one man wounded. Lt Avery to hospital.	All.
	22		Work continued as on previous day.	All.
CAMP 16	23	at 3-30 p.m.	Battery was relieved by 10th T.M.B. Marched to MAUREPAS - thence by bus to CAMP 16.	All.
	24		Men engaged on bringing kits from MARICOURT to CAMP 16.	All.
	25		XMAS DAY. Battery paraded for Divine Service at 11 A.M.	All.
	26		Men employed on fatigues - some on drying gun boots - others at Ammunition Dumps.	All.
	27		All available men continued work at Ammunition Dumps under Ordnance Supervision.	All.

Army Form C. 2118.

WAR DIARY
or
INTELLIGENCE SUMMARY
(Erase heading not required.)

Place	Date	Hour	Summary of Events and Information	Remarks and references to Appendices
SAILLY-LAURETTE	1916 Dec 28		Battery marches to rest billets in SAILLY-LAURETTE. Billets found to be very uncomfortable.	M.A.
	29		O.C. obtained new billets for men. Horse lines completed and, in spite of rain, no shortage. Training, ground and range reconnoitered. All huts inspected.	M.A.
	30		Officers of the Battery inspected by O.C. Billets inspected. Capt. Ralph Roberts officers of the R.F.A. mortar-shells to be observed while at rest.	M.A.
	31		N.C.O.s on various points of discipline to be observed while at rest. Box respirators inspected by Divisional Gas Officer. Shrewd parade.	S.M.

SECRET

WAR DIARY

OF

12ᵀᴴ TRENCH MORTAR BATTERY

From 1ˢᵗ JANUARY 1917
To 31ˢᵗ JANUARY 1917

31ˢᵗ JANUARY 1917

J.A. Roberts Capt.
Commanding
12 Trench Mortar Battery

Army Form C. 2118.

WAR DIARY
or
INTELLIGENCE SUMMARY
(Erase heading not required.)

Instructions regarding War Diaries and Intelligence Summaries are contained in F. S. Regs., Part II. and the Staff Manual respectively. Title Pages will be prepared in manuscript.

Place	Date	Hour	Summary of Events and Information	Remarks and references to Appendices
SAILLY LAURETTE	1917 JAN 1		Training - Physical Training at 7.15AM. Bayonet fighting, arm and Squad drill, and musketry during morning. Gun drill and lectures in the afternoon.	Nil.
	2.		Training - as on 1st	Nil.
	3.		Training - as on 1st	Nil.
	4.		Training - as on 1st	Nil.
	5.		Training during the morning. Football during afternoon	Nil
	6.		Training during morning. Brass helmets near pattern No 1 & No 2 section were issued to BATTERY.	Nil
	7.		Divisional Xmas day. Dinner Service in Camp 12.4. and 10 A.M. Dinners at 1 P.M. Battery Concert at 6.30 P.M.	Nil.
	8.		No 1. Section fired on range during morning. No 2 went for a route march. Football in afternoon - No 1 & 2 Scotland V England men and restmen.	Nil.
	9.		No 2. Section fired on range. No 1. routmarched. Lectures and gun drill in afternoon	Nil.
	10.		Unit training during morning Runnaby in afternoon	Nil
	11.		Battery fired on range during morning. Football in afternoon Battery v 12"H.G.Cy. etc.	Nil

2449   Wt. W14957/M90 750,000 1/16 J.B.C. & A. Forms/C.2118/12.

Army Form C. 2118.

WAR DIARY
or
INTELLIGENCE SUMMARY

(Erase heading not required.)

Instructions regarding War Diaries and Intelligence Summaries are contained in F. S. Regs., Part II. and the Staff Manual respectively. Title Pages will be prepared in manuscript.

Place	Date	Hour	Summary of Events and Information	Remarks and references to Appendices
SALLY-LAURETTE	1917 Jan 12		Training	WH
	13		Changing of bivvies	WH
	14		Church Parade in Camp 124.	WH
	15		Training.	WH
	16		Training in morning. Football in afternoon. Battery v Lance Fus.	WH
	17		No Athletics. Thaw made it for snow.	
	18		Training - Rest & sport in morning. Kit inspection and lecture afternoon. Athletics used on terms	WH
	19		Dispatch rider's nomination put forward. Bgde Boxing Competition continued. Training in morning. Football in afternoon.	WH
	20		Cleaning sollets. Kit inspection during morning. Bombers tested in barracks pm.	WH
	21		during afternoon. Football No 1 v No 2 section. Divine Service in 124 Camp at 11 AM. Battery concert in billets at 6:30 PM.	WH
	22		Battery first about 200 rounds on range. J.O.C. Brigade war scheme. Operation Orders received for move on 23rd.	WH
BRAY	23		Battery marched to BRAY via Bray neck. Brigade HQ leaving Sally-Laurette at 9:30 AM. Amendment received to Operation Order of 22nd regarding line of march on 24 h.	WH
SUZANNE	24		Battery left BRAY at 2:30 PM and marched with Brigade HQ to SUZANNE. Lt Handcock with Rect Car Kit sent to Camp 112.	WH
	25		Weather raining. Old training continued.	WH
	26		Training	WH

Army Form C. 2118.

WAR DIARY
or
INTELLIGENCE SUMMARY
(Erase heading not required.)

Place	Date	Hour	Summary of Events and Information	Remarks and references to Appendices
SUSANNE	1917 JAN 27th		Training continued. Warning order for relief of 11th Bde received	W/1
	28th		Divine Service with L.T. in SUSANNE	S/1
	29th		Spare kit moved by battery from Camp 112 to Bn.Y.1.C. erected 11"T.M.B. in camp near CORLU.	T/1
	30		Operation order for relief or limit of T.M. movements. 2/Lt MATSON went up the line to reconnoitre gun positions, as 11"T.M.B. have not pers. unit to visit side sector owing to state of the trenches 11"T.M.B. in huts	M/1
CURLU RAVINE	31.		Battery marched from SUSANNE at 8.45 A.M. and reported in CURLU RAVINE	B/1

SECRET.

WAR DIARY.

OF

12TH T. M. B.

FROM: 1ST FEBRUARY 1917.

TO: 28TH FEBRUARY 1917.

F. O. Roberts CAPTAIN
COMMANDING 12TH TRENCH MORTAR BATTERY.

DATE
2/3/17

WAR DIARY or INTELLIGENCE SUMMARY

Army Form C. 2118.

(Erase heading not required.)

Place	Date	Hour	Summary of Events and Information	Remarks and references to Appendices
CURLU	1917 FEB. 1		O.C. and 2nd Lt MATSON went to Bde. H.Q. at Junction Wood.	
	2.		O.C. reconnoitred line as far as BOUCHAVESNES and THE DUMP. 2nd Lt returned 11th Bde.	
	3.		O.C. received orders at Bde H.Q. to move into line on following day.	
MARRIÈRES WOOD.	4.		Bde in MARRIÈRES WOOD relieved by Capt. ROBERTS during morning. 2nd Lt MATSON took two gun teams left Curlu at 1 P.M. and marched to R.E. Wood to arrange details of accommodation for Battery. Remainder of Battery less reserves proceeded to new camp at 10 P.M.	
	5.		Guns were brought to MARRIÈRES Wood by reserves. Battery was employed on improvement of dug-out and bivouac accommodation and in carrying French ammunition.	
	6.		No 1 Section employed on carrying material for R.E. No 2 Section on making & continued work on dugouts. Lt Avery reported for duty.	
	7.		Work continued for R.E. Remainder of Battery continued work on dug-outs. 2nd Lt MATSON at C.T. AVERY reconnoitred work in MARRIÈRES Wood for Bde.	
	8.		Party continued work for R.E. 100 Rounds ammunition cleaned. Work on dug-outs continued	

WAR DIARY
or
INTELLIGENCE SUMMARY

Army Form C. 2118.

Place	Date 1917	Hour	Summary of Events and Information	Remarks and references to Appendices
HARRIERS WOOD	9		Work on dugouts and for R.E. continued. 100 Rounds Ammunition unloaded	CIHA
	10		Lt Matson took two guns into right sector. 100 Rounds ammunition brought to Quarry. 47 Rounds expended	CIHA
	11		Prepared 225 rounds for transport and one gun of L.T.M. Battery brought up to Quarry. Lt Avery regrouping two guns on left of RIGHT SECTOR. 25 Rounds expended	CIHA
	12		Operation order recd. re Inter-Brigade relief to take place on 15th inst. Guns taken into line to put up flank barrages for a raid. Enemy bombarded front and support trenches from 7 – 7.30 p.m. with 77mm & 150mm shells. Raid cancelled till 8 p.m. 157 rounds fired during the night at enemies wire in right sector. A working party was dispersed by gun in right sector. Lt Irwin relieved Lt Matson in line.	CIHA
	13		Working party (15 men) employed in deepening support trench in left sector. No firing on that army to working parties.	CIHA
	14		24 rounds fired at wire. C.T. and suspected M.G. emplacement. Enemies working party fired at and apparently dispersed. Officer from 11th T.M.B. taken over position of.	CIHA
	15		92 rounds fired on wire. Working party of 20 men attached to party from Lancs. Fus. marched.	CIHA
SUZANNE	16		Relieved by 11th T.M.B. to Camp 16 Suzanne. Weather much warmer – thawing fast.	CIHA

Army Form C. 2118.

WAR DIARY
or
INTELLIGENCE SUMMARY
(Erase heading not required.)

Instructions regarding War Diaries and Intelligence Summaries are contained in F. S. Regs., Part II. and the Staff Manual respectively. Title Pages will be prepared in manuscript.

Place	Date	Hour	Summary of Events and Information	Remarks and references to Appendices
SUZANNE	1917 FEB 17		Men on camp fatigues. Camp visited at work by B.G.C Bde	OMA
	— 18		Warning order recd re move to CORBIE. Men fitted. N.C.O. sent to Bde Training School	OMA
	— 19		Clothing inspected	OMA
	— 20		Rain. Moved to Camp 117 leaving SUZANNE at 9.15 arriving 12.0 AE on	OMA
Camp 117	— 21		Marched to CORBIE leaving at 9.28 arriving 1.0 PM. Trench maps called in	OMA
CORBIE	— 22		Rifles & Kit inspected — Squad drill	OMA
	— 23		Marched to LA NEUVILLE training area — Squad drill, Musketry, Rifle Exercise	OMA
	— 24		Parade as above	OMA
	— 25		Parade — P.T., Bayonet fighting, Rifle exercises, Squad drill, Lecture.	OMA
	— 26		Parade as above — Training grounds allotted at FOUILLOY	OMA
	— 27		Parade as above	OMA
	— 28		Parade as above	OMA

<u>SECRET</u>

WAR DIARY

OF

12TH. T.M.B.

From 1ST March 1917
To 31ST March 1917.

Date 3-4-17. J.D.Roberts Commanding

"12TH" Trench Mortar Battery.

Army Form C. 2118.

WAR DIARY
or
INTELLIGENCE SUMMARY
(Erase heading not required.)

Instructions regarding War Diaries and Intelligence Summaries are contained in F.S. Regs, Part II. and the Staff Manual respectively. Title Pages will be prepared in manuscript.

Place	Date	Hour	Summary of Events and Information	Remarks and references to Appendices
CORBIE	1917 MARCH 1		Fine weather. Paraded 7.35, 9-12, 2-3. W.O. received to be prepared to move at 48 hours notice	OPH
	2		Fine. Parade 7.15-7.45, 9-12, 2-3	OPH
	3		Fine. Parade 7.15-7.45, 9-12, 2-3. W.O. re Move received at 4 PM., O.O. No 11 received at 7.30 PM	CPH
	4		Fine. Paraded 7.15-7.45, 9-12, 2-3. Left CORBIE at 8 AM, passed starting point at 9.9 AM, Halted 11.50-1.20 for dinners. Arrived MORTAINVILLE at 3.15 PM. Cpl Garside transferred to 3rd Brighton School. O.O. No 12 received.	CPH / CPH
BEAUVAL	5		Fine. Left MORTAINVILLE at 8.30 AM, arriving at BEAUVAL at 1.30. O.O. No 13 received.	CPH
REMAISNIL	6		Left BEAUVAL at 8.30 morning REMAISNIL at 2.40 PM. O.O. No 14 received.	OPH
	7		Fine. Left REMAISNIL at 8 AM arriving at BOUFFLERS at 1.30 PM. Foot inspection at 3.30	CPH
BOUFFLERS	8		Inspection of clothing, rifles and gas helmets. G.O.C.'s conference. Red cloth grenade issued and worn on should of tunics	CPH
	9		Fine. Parade 7.15-7.45, 9-12.30 N.C.O.'s Lecture 2-3	OPH
	10		Fine. Parades 7.15-7.45, 9-12.30 Football in afternoon	CPH
	11		Showery. Church parade RCs at 11 AM C of E at 5 PM hrs. 6.0 PM.	CPH
	12		1 Officer 1 Sgt 2 cpls and 16 men arrived as reinforcements, bringing battery strength to 25-8 over establishment. Fine weather. Parade 7.15-7.45, 9-12.30 Football 2.30-4	OPH
	13		Dull. Parades as above. Red grenade on sleeve replaced by 3" equilateral triangle point downwards.	CPH
	14		Fine. Parades as above.	OPH
	15		Fine. Parades as above. G.O.C.'s Conference at 2 PM	CPH
	16		Showery. Parades as above.	OPH

WAR DIARY or INTELLIGENCE SUMMARY

Army Form C. 2118.

Place	Date	Hour	Summary of Events and Information	Remarks and references to Appendices
BOUFFLERS	1917 MARCH 17		Fine weather. Parades 7:15-7:45, 9-12:30, 2-3:30. 3 men from reinforcements returned to their units on 17th.	X/M
	18		Rain. Church parade 4:0 pm. 3 men arrived to replace men returned to units on 17th.	C/M
	19		Rain. Parades 9-12:30, 2-3:30. Night operations cancelled owing to weather. W.O. received re. attack.	O/M
	20		Fine. 7:15-7:45 Running drill 9-12:30 attack practice. W.O. received to be prepared to move at 24 hour notice.	C/M
	21		O.O. received re. move to 17th Corps area. Rain. Parades 7:15-7:45, 9-12:30, 2-3.	O/M
ORLENCOURT	22		Left BOUFFLERS at 11 AM. Entrained at AUX-LE-CHATEAU at 3 PM, marched from the RAILHEAD ROELLECOURT to ORLENCOURT arriving at 9 PM. Rain + storm.	C/M
	23		Snow. Army carrying our stores not arriving, had to borrow truck from 2nd Pack.	C/M
	24		Rain. Parades 9-12:30, 2-4. Stores arrived	C/M
	25		Fine. Church parade 10 AM at MONCHY BRETON. Detail of attack on Béarmoy Brancion Fuze rec'd. 50 trans. Ammunition rec'd.	O/M
	26		Sun and rain. OO 18 received. Return.	O/M
	27		Fine. Parades 7:15-7:45, 9-12:30, football 2-3. 6 carriers attached to battery from 7th Halions.	O/M
	28		Fine. Route March 9-12:30. Two subsection practice attack with Gun No.1 and N.O.1 of 2nd sub.	O/M
	29		Battery reconnoitred forward area. Heavy rain. Practice attack with 7th Halions.	O/M
	30		Rain. Parades 8:30-12:30. Range set up at U3c,d (36BSW 20W) 2/Lt IRWIN and 2 runners attempted firing.	C/M
	31		Fine. High wind. Gun's demonstration attack on range, firing 15B rounds from guns at "strong point".	O/M

SECRET

WAR DIARY

OF

12ᵀᴴ T.M.B.

FROM 1ˢᵀ APRIL 1917
TO 30ᵀᴴ APRIL 1917

[signature] Lieut.
COMMANDING 12ᵀʰ T.M.B.

2-5-17.

Army Form C. 2118.

WAR DIARY
or
INTELLIGENCE SUMMARY

(Erase heading not required.)

Instructions regarding War Diaries and Intelligence Summaries are contained in F. S. Regs., Part II. and the Staff Manual respectively. Title Pages will be prepared in manuscript.

Place	Date	Hour	Summary of Events and Information	Remarks and references to Appendices
ORLENCOURT	1917 APRIL 1		Church Parades C of E 11.10 Wes. 10.15 R C 10.45. detail of ballistic rings read. Weather Fine	OHA
	2		Parades 7.15-7.45 P.T. 9-12 Rifle firing on range near MONCHY BRETON 2-3.30 Gas practice W.O. rec'd re move to Y camp. Major Irvine. Weather cold, snow in afternoon	EHA
	3		Heavy snowfall. Lectures.	EH
	4		Fine weather. 8.30-12.30 Practice attack with Brigade. 2-3 Lecture. Lt Hughes and 2 NCOs reconnoitred forward area. Major O.O. rec'd.	EH
	5		Fine. 9-12.30 Practice attack. Bde. inspect by GOC/Corps W.O. rec'd to move on 6th move for 1 gun and 24 hrs. All guns thrown by packmules	EH
	6		9-12.30 Attack practice firing 50 rounds By OVS OC No 17 rec'd Gas helmets inspected by Bde. gas N.C.O.	EH
Y Camp	7		Left ORLENCOURT at 11 AM arriving at Y camp at 4 PM. Weather fine	EH
	8		Weather fine. Lt Hughes + 6 men sent to assembly area to reconnoitre shells. 2 hills grenades issued out to each man. New B.A.B. Code recd. Guns to under came under orders of Batn commanders at 6 P.M. - Lt Anvery with three guns of No.1 Section of Kings Own. Lt Irwin with one gun of No 2 Section to Essex Regt and Sgt McCullough with one gun of No 2 Section to Lanc. Fus. Zero hour received.	EH

Army Form C. 2118.

WAR DIARY
or
INTELLIGENCE SUMMARY
(Erase heading not required.)

Place	Date	Hour	Summary of Events and Information	Remarks and references to Appendices
Y CAMP	April 9 1917		Gun teams paraded with battalions to which they were attached viz. No. 1, 2 & 3 under Lt AVERY with KING'S OWN, No. 5 under 2Lt IRWIN with ESSEX and No. 6 under Sgt McCULLOUGH with LANCS F.S. ESSEX left Y CAMP at 3.10 A.M. LANCS FUS. and KING'S OWN following at 15 minutes intervals. Tanks carried accompanied Lst gun team. On arrival at Assembly Area - WEST of ST NICHOLAS - Lst team was provided carriers drew four shells each from Dump and teams took over their guns which had come up on a limber. The BRIGADE moved from ASSEMBLY AREA at 10 AM to meet up to BROWN LINE whilst was kept every position and about 300 ft behind the original front line. Soon after crossing enemy original front line, the BRIGADE halted for an hour and a half to allow troops of the 9th Division to pass through. During this time LT AVERY and two men were wounded and one gun was put out of action. The march to BROWN LINE was concluded almost without incident, the enemy's barrage being very feeble. The BRIGADE passed through the 9th Division to the attack at 3.10 PM. The first objective a strong point about 200 ft in front of BROWN LINE was carried easily, very little resistance being encountered. The BRIGADE halted here for half an hour. CPL NEEDHAM now in command of 2 remaining guns of KING'S OWN reported to O.C. DUKES who were to pass through the former REGT and were ordered to consolidate on that line - "4th GERMAN SYSTEM"	

WAR DIARY or INTELLIGENCE SUMMARY

REF FRANCE 57th Bn

Place	Date	Hour	Summary of Events and Information	Remarks and references to Appendices
CAMP	1917 9th April		- CONT.D The BRIGADE continued the advance to the GREEN LINE - the first objective. On the right the DUKES captured FAMPOUX and dug in on EASTERN edge of the village. The LANCS FUS in the centre and ESSEX REGT on the left advanced to a thousand yards and consolidated a line running north from FAMPOUX to HYDERABAD REDOUBT. up to the present little serious resistance was encountered and none of the guns came into action. The gun park LANCS FUS and ESSEX began on advanced positions but found no targets with range. Excepting to minds all ammunition taken in assembly area reached final positions. Positions occupied on the forenoon were from three to four hundred yards short of pre-arranged GREEN LINE BATTERY H.Q.RS moved forward with the attack and were established at H.14.b.3.2.	Appx 1
H.22.a.8.8	10		BATTERY H.Q. moved forward to H.22 & S.F. took up a position at H.15.a.b. Good harassed fire in front of CORPS H.Q. Enemy noticed digging in and DUKES attacked GREEN LINE under thoroughly of STOKES and MACHINE GUNS. Attack failed owing to long range R.G. fire.	Appx II

Army Form C. 2118.

WAR DIARY
or
INTELLIGENCE SUMMARY
(Erase heading not required.)

R.E.F. FRANCE 2000 51 BNW

Place	Date	Hour	Summary of Events and Information	Remarks and references to Appendices
12 a 8.6.	April 10		At 10 A.M. No 6 Gun advanced with Lan Fus to GREEN LINE where it went dug in. The gun during the day fired on enemy working in H.19 & 20. During the night the gun hung fire. EASTERN end of FAMPOUX was shot out of action and Capt Roberts withdrew Lan Fus Gun and sent it to replace the gun in FAMPOUX. No 3 Gun what was in 4th GERMAN SYSTEM was also ment up to support attack which was to take place on following morning.	8MM
	11		At 12 noon KINGS OWN and DUKES again attacked GREEN LINE No 3 & 6 Guns provided barrage fire. Objective was reached and consolidated. At 12 noon O.C. withdrew No 5. Gun from ESSEX front. 27 R.W.F. took command of Nos 3 & 6 Guns in FAMPOUX and gave fresh dug in at RAILWAY EMBANKMENT H18 at 2.2. at mid night 11-12	8MM

Army Form C. 2118.

WAR DIARY
or
INTELLIGENCE SUMMARY
(Erase heading not required.)

Instructions regarding War Diaries and Intelligence Summaries are contained in F. S. Regs., Part II. and the Staff Manual respectively. Title Pages will be prepared in manuscript.

Place	Date 1917	Hour	Summary of Events and Information	Remarks and references to Appendices
TAMPOUX	APRIL 11		Essex Gun under 2/Lt IRWIN was withdrawn to Batty H.Q. as the enemy were out of range. Two remaining guns under 2/Lt IRWIN Coy to at Railway ARCH H.18.d.2.2. to support KINGS OWN Infantry attacked and gained some ground.	B/1.
H.14.a.	12		9th Division attacked ROEUX — GAVRELLE ROAD. Brigade came into reserve and all guns were withdrawn to BROWN LINE and RAILWAY (H.14.a.) 2/Lt HUGHES reported from Y CAMP.	J/11
H 14 a	13		Order rec'd to move back to G.11 on following day.	Sept.
G.11	14		Battery paraded at 8.30 A.M. and marched to G.11 where accommodation was found in original front and support lines.	Sept
G.11	15		11 horses were brought from Y CAMP to replace casualties and reduce some of the teams. B.O.R. returned to Y CAMP.	Sept.
G.11	16		Warning order received to be prepared to move to the line on 18th. Guns cleaned	J/11

Army Form C. 2118.

WAR DIARY
or
INTELLIGENCE SUMMARY

(Erase heading not required.)

Instructions regarding War Diaries and Intelligence Summaries are contained in F.S. Regs., Part II. and the Staff Manual respectively. Title Pages will be prepared in manuscript.

Place	Date	Hour	Summary of Events and Information	Remarks and references to Appendices
FRANCE ST. B. NO.	1917 APRIL 17		3 boxes of ballistite rings recd. for miniature range.	Appx
G. 11	18	10 A.M.	W.O. recd re attack by Division S. of GAVRELLE. Rifle inspection at 10 A.M. Weather very wet. Operation Order No 29 recd.	Sept.
G. 11	19		O.O. No.29 recd. cancelled. W.O. that Brigade would be relieved on following day recd. O.O. re move recd.	Appt.
MONTAN-ESCOURT	20		Battery paraded at 10.30 AM and marched to MONTANESCOURT. W.O. received re move on 21st	Appy Appt
MANIN	21		O.O. recd. Battery passed starting point at 10.20 AM and marched to MANIN. O.O. recd re move on 22	
BEAU-FORT	22		Battery was inspected by G.O.C. Brigade at 10.30 AM. and marched to BEAUFORT passing starting point at 10.45 AM. W.O. recd re move on 23rd	Appt.
LE CAUROY	23		O.O. recd. Battery passed starting point at 12.20 PM and marched to LE CAUROY.	Appt.
	24	9 AM	Muster parade at 9 AM. Men employed bringing kits etc. from BEAUFORT in handcarts	Sept.
	25		Physical training + Close Order Drill during morning. Baths at 12 noon at OPPY. O.O. re move recd.	Appt
	26		Battery paraded at 9.30 AM and marched to SARS-LEZ-BOIS	Appt

2449 Wt. W14957/M90 750,000 1/16 J.B.C. & A. Forms/C.2118/12.

WAR DIARY
or
INTELLIGENCE SUMMARY

Ref. Lens 11 and 51 B N.W.

Place	Date 1917	Hour	Summary of Events and Information	Remarks and references to Appendices
Spr: Les. (Posh)	April 27	1.0	No. 34 n.c.o. Inspection of Anti-Gas Appliances and Close-order drill during forenoon. O.O. No. 35 nil. N. move.	234.
Tilloy-les-Hermaville	28		Battery passed starting point at 10.15 AM and marched to Tilloy-lez-Hermaville. Brigade conference at 5 P.M. Capt. Roberts went to hospital and 2/Lt Irwin took over command of battery. O.O. and amendment received. N. move.	2c/11
G.17	29.		Battery paraded at 6.15 AM and marched to Camp in G.17 - West of St Nicholas. 2/Lt Hervey was attached for duty with Battery. 2/Lt Bee to Lez B'de.	441
Hervin Villiers	30		2/Lt Irwin visited the line. Brigade conference at 3 P.M. - details of forthcoming attack discussed. C.O. order re relief by 12 R.B. of 103rd Brigade rec'd. Battery forward 'SL' at 9 P.M. and relieved 102nd T.M.B in line. Relief complete at 3 A.M. on 1st May	M.1

SECRET

Seen by
G.O.C.
B.M.
S.C.

WAR DIARY

OF

12TH. T.M.B.

PERIOD,

FROM 1ST. OCTOBER, 1917.

TO 31ST OCTOBER, 1917.

C.L. Matson Lieut.
Commanding 12th Trench Mortar Battery

Army Form C. 2118.

WAR DIARY
or
INTELLIGENCE SUMMARY
(Erase heading not required.)

HAZEBROUCK 5A 20SWB 28

Instructions regarding War Diaries and Intelligence Summaries are contained in F. S. Regs., Part II. and the Staff Manual respectively. Title Pages will be prepared in manuscript.

Place	Date	Hour	Summary of Events and Information	Remarks and references to Appendices
28. C.6.3.1.	1/12/17		Great artillery activity on both sides	J.M.
			Relieved by 11" T.M.B	
			Relief complete 8 p.m.	
			Arrived SOLFERINO CAMP 11.30 pm	
B23 16.5	2/12/17	5.10 pm	Working party up the line	J.M.
	3/12/17		Inspection of gas appliances	J.M.
	4/12/17		O.O. 69 received	J.M.
			P.T. + drill	
	5/12/17		P.T. drill. Baths.	J.M.
	6/12/17		O.O. 70 received	J.M.
			P.T. + drill	

Army Form C. 2118.

WAR DIARY
or
INTELLIGENCE SUMMARY

(Erase heading not required.)

SHEET 28 Reg 100 SHELL RD

Instructions regarding War Diaries and Intelligence Summaries are contained in F.S. Regs, Part II. and the Staff Manual respectively. Title Pages will be prepared in manuscript.

Place	Date	Hour	Summary of Events and Information	Remarks and references to Appendices
Bx ABS.	7/10/17		O.O. 71 received Church Parade.	guns
	8/10/17		Battery went into kit. H.Q. + 2 Guns to BIRD Ho. 2 gun to LOUIS Fm. One under orders of Essex the other and LweCos. J24 c59	guns
SaoVor-98 Southampton	9/10/17	5.15am	Zero hour Guns not called into action	guns
	10/10/17	8.0 pm	Zero gun at LOUIS Fm withdrawn to transport lines at BRIDGE June 8.20 p.m. Enemy shelled with gas shell	guns
	11/10/17	8.0 am	Trench Great artillery activity	guns

Army Form C. 2118.

WAR DIARY
or
INTELLIGENCE SUMMARY
(Erase heading not required.)

Instructions regarding War Diaries and Intelligence Summaries are contained in F.S. Regs., Part II and the Staff Manual respectively. Title Pages will be prepared in manuscript.

BELGIUM Sheet 28 1/20000 2 & B

Place	Date	Hour	Summary of Events and Information	Remarks and references to Appendices
S30 d 77 - 9.3	4/10/17	6.30	Zero. 7.0 guns withdrawn from BOAT HOUSE to CANAL BANK	Suy
	5/10/17		7.0 guns withdrawn from Canal Bank to BRIDGE Junc.	Suy
			H.Q. withdrawn from here to BRIDGE Junc. 0.0.75 received.	
B30 b 45	14/10/17		Battery left BRIDGE Junc at 11.30 —	Suy
			Battery detrained at ROUEN & marched to PITT C.10	
			0.0.76 received	
	15/10/17		Company in etc. Baths at Le COUTROYE	Suy
	16/10/17		Left PITT C.10 at 10-30 — marched to ST JAN TER BIEZEN	
H.Q. at L6I S.6	17/10/17		Administrative Instructions No 7 received	Suy

WAR DIARY
INTELLIGENCE SUMMARY

BELGIUM FRANCE Summary 27 Jun 11

Place	Date	Hour	Summary of Events and Information	Remarks and references to Appendices
LS d 5-6	18/4/17		Left St Jan Ter Biezen at 3.30 p.m. marched to Hopoutre entrained & left at 7.30 p.m.	J.M.
	19/4/17		detrained AUBIGNY at 1.30 & marched to MONTENESCOURT	J.M.
MONTENESCOURT	20/4/17	9.10 10.11	Reveille. P.T. inspection of gas appliances & cleaning equipment.	J.M.
	21/4/17		Church Parade	J.M.
	22.10.17		Running drill Close Order drill 4 P.Y. football O.O No. 78 received	J.M.
	23.10.17		Running drill Close Order drill Lecture Close Order Drill Batn marched to billets in ARRAS, leaving MONESCOURT at 2.45 p.m. & arriving at ARRAS at 5.30 pm	J.M.
G 27h. 9.0	24.10.17			J.M.

Army Form C. 2118.

WAR DIARY
or
INTELLIGENCE SUMMARY
(Erase heading not required.)

FRANCE 5

Place	Date	Hour	Summary of Events and Information	Remarks and references to Appendices
G27 b 90	25.10.17		Close Order Drill. Inspection of Boots, Clothing etc. Bayonet aux Close Order Drill.	
	26.10.17		O.B. no 79 received	A/M
	27.10.17		Close Order Drill. Inspection of Emeri etc. Appliances, & Gas Drill	A/M
	28.10.17		Church Parade	A/M
	29.10.17		24 men arrived for instruction in Trench Mortar Drill as usual. J.A.V. School started.	A/M
	30.10.17		Drill as usual	A/M
	31.10.17		Drill as usual. G.O. 80 received	A/M

SECRET

WAR DIARY

OF

12TH T.M.B.

PERIOD:-

FROM 1ST NOVEMBER 1917
TO 30TH NOVEMBER 1917.

Gordon L Smith Capt.
Com'ding 12th. Trench Mortar Battery.

3.12.17.

Army Form C. 2118.

WAR DIARY
or
INTELLIGENCE SUMMARY

(Erase heading not required.)

Instructions regarding War Diaries and Intelligence Summaries are contained in F. S. Regs., Part II. and the Staff Manual respectively. Title Pages will be prepared in manuscript.

REF SHEET 51.8.

Place	Date	Hour	Summary of Events and Information	Remarks and references to Appendices
ARRAS	1st. March	9am	Close order drill & Bayonet fighting. Firing on Range (Osten) at G.32.a.	GRO
	2nd	9am	Parades as usual	GRO
	3rd	9am	Gas inspection — Arm & Clothing inspection. Baths.	GRO
	4th	9am	Church Parades. CAPT J.B. IRWIN reported (from leave)	GRO
	5th	9am	Close order drill bayonet fighting. Physical Training.	GRO
	6th	9am	Parades as usual. Operation Order No/81 rec'd	GRO
	7th	9am	Route march. Close order drill & P.T.	GRO
	8th	9am	Fatigues	GRO
		12.45	Parade for trenches.	
Msa.00.80		4.30pm	Maj. Sutton arrives & Maj. Hughes relieved. 11th. TMB. in DALE TRENCH.	GRO
	9th	6am	Guns were registered on SOS lines on enemy front line LONG TRENCH & SPOON TRENCH. Fifty rounds trench mortar fire carried out on German front system. Hostile shelling was very quiet on the whole front system.	GRO
	10th	6am	Operation Order No/82 issued. During the night 25 rounds were fired on SPOON TRENCH. O86. 10 rounds were fired on the MOUND O8c1.6. & 20 rounds on LONG TR O2d.6.7. The enemy fired about 30 light T.M./s in 4 occurred VIMY AVE. — DALE TR & MOUND A/104 men shelled during the day.	GRO
	11th	6am	Harassing fire (55 rounds) were carried out on the Enemy system SPOON & LONG TRENCH.	GRO
	12th	6am	Four Gun pits in Hill Support revetted & camouflaged. Chalk foundations were laid in pit bottoms.	GRO

WAR DIARY or INTELLIGENCE SUMMARY

Army Form C. 2118.

(Erase heading not required.)

REF SHEET 51B

Place	Date	Hour	Summary of Events and Information	Remarks and references to Appendices
N5a.00.80	12th	10.30pm	Operation Order IV/63 ref/ Pursuit Scheme.	A.P.1
	13th	6am	Enemy shelled front system in early morning. Retaliatory fire was carried out by our Stokes Mortars. Our MGs were very active during the night. Enemy fired Gas (lethal) shells on our front system about VINE AVENUE & HILL SUPPORT.	A.P.1
	14th	6am	Our TMs fired hourly on the MOUNDS O2d6.f. Barrages being fired. 35 rounds were fired on BOLT & SPOON TR.	A.P.1
		9.50am	Enemy fired 20 rounds on CANISTER & DALE TR from direction of BOIS de VERT.	
		7am/11pm	Enemy fired 5 about 8 Light & Heavy TMs on Support line, 6 active being counted. During the night harassing fires were carried out on the enemy front system.	
	15th	6am	Enemy Artillery were more active than usual. Barrages were fired by Stokes Mortars in SPOON TR. O&6.8.9 & O&6.6. Enemy TMs were less active than usual, a few rounds fell near our Support lines. Stokes Mortars co-operated in a raid by Leins Fus. at 9am. Our intense barrage was placed on enemy front line (Northern boundary O26.35.20 Southern boundary O20b0.75) from Zero to Zero + 2. From Zero + 25 mins to Zero + 26 the barrage was repeated. 20 rounds per gun per minute.	A.P.1
	16th	6am	From 12-2pm Our artillery were active on enemy's front line & communications. Our Light TMs fired 37 rounds on SPOON & LONG TR Hostile activity N.1. No.2 Section made off Souft returned No.1 Section made 2/Lt Hough.	
DALE TRENCH		about 4.30pm	Battery HQ temporarily established in DALE TR Operation Order O0B6 no	
	17th	6am	Our Artillery were active throughout the day on enemy front line & one. Our Heavy TMs were now entering on SPOON & LONG TR. From 10am - 12.30pm Enemy light Battery	A.P.1

2449 Wt. W14957/Mg0 750,000 1/16 J.B.C. & A. Forms/C.2118/12.

WAR DIARY
or
INTELLIGENCE SUMMARY

Army Form C. 2118.

(Erase heading not required.)

REF SB SHEET

Place	Date	Hour	Summary of Events and Information	Remarks and references to Appendices
#D4LETR	17th	7.15pm	Light Stokes TMs co-operated in a raid on junction of HEM & LONG TR trench. Kings Own Artillery was placed on enemy front line at this point from Zero to Zero + 2 minutes. Enemy retaliation was slight.	Apl.
N5a 00.60	18th	6.50pm	Enemy fired heavy TMs on front line MOUND ALLEY / VM AVENUE to Zero + 110.	
		6am	Artillery MGs & TMs were active throughout the day. At Zero 3pm the Stokes Mortar fired 300 rounds on LONG TR co-operating with Artillery MGs & Smoke Barrage on whole Corps front. Baby Hy. active at N5a 00.80. Enemy trench Mortar very active throughout the pressed particularly between hours 9am -11am & 2pm-5pm.	Apl.
	19th	6am	One Artillery was active on enemy forward system. Stokes Mortar very active at LONG of the MOUND during the day. One EA patrolled our line until 12.45 p.m. 2nd Lieut Hogarth 1st K.O. Regt + 2nd Lt Horstick 2nd Rifles reported on TMB for duty.	Apl.
	20th	6pm	Our Artillery MGs + TMs were active at 6.20 am in conjunction with a raid by the Brigade on our right. Stokes Mortar fired in accordance with orders. The guns were unable to fire owing to muzzle discharge, & all were carefully hampered by the smoke particularly when dealing with misfires. Enemy big LTTMs were active on our front system throughout the day. Rifle Grenades also were discharged. Enemy FA flew our own line about 7mm & again at 3.30 p.m. Visibility was very poor. Rockets ascending into 2 or 4 green by LB were used to call barrage for. Enemy were very far up LB during night.	Apl.
	21st	6am	Our 60 pdr Artillery retaliated for enemy gas bombardment on our left between 12.30-12.45 p.m. Stokes Mortars fired 155 rounds in the following target @ 03.00 on exploding dump Conder TR between 12.00 M1AN + 220 MM. Enemy's position behind spoon+LONG TR B21 90-20. German front line N+S of B20/20.35. This was engaged between 2.45 p.m. + 3.15 p.m. & again at enemy stand to. Enemy were evidently perturbed & sent up numerous white lights.	

Army Form C. 2118.

WAR DIARY
or
INTELLIGENCE SUMMARY
(Erase heading not required.)

Instructions regarding War Diaries and Intelligence Summaries are contained in F.S. Regs., Part II. and the Staff Manual respectively. Title Pages will be prepared in manuscript.

Place	Date Nov	Hour	Summary of Events and Information	Remarks and references to Appendices
M5a 00.80	21st	5.30am to 6am	Enemy barrage in front of support line. Enemy M.G.'s active throughout period. Enemy E.A. flew low over front system firing in trenches.	GR1
	22nd	6 pm	One 3" Stokes Mortar fired on enemy wire in front of SPOON Tr. between O.8.b.70.95 – O.8.b.70.70. Shots were observed to fall in enemy wire with good effect. 6" NEWTON Stokes fired on enemy wire. 3" Stokes were again fired on wire between O.8.b.70.95 – O.8.b.70.10. Enemy Artillery observed 30 rounds were fired at 4.30 p.m. SADDLE SUPPORT being shelled. Light barrage.	GR1 Casualties 3 O.R.
	23rd	6 am	2.30 p.m. 7 wounds at 4.30 pm. Especially between 5.15am - 6.0am Enemy artillery active throughout the day. G.R.Smith 9/4 A5A was commenced J.13.A.7.11.13 from J.B.I.Owen Capt. Two E.A. flew over our lines between 11 A.M & 11.30 A.M. G.R.Smith 9/4 A5A was commenced O.8.b.70.95 & O.8.b.70.10. 3" Stokes were active throughout day anything seen in front of SPOON Tr. between O.8.b.70.95 & O.8.b.70.10. Enemy fired eleven a light barrage in our cutting. 6" Newtons co-operated. 160 rounds were fired. One E.A. flew over our line at 6am 23.11.17. & again at 11 am. SADDLE & HILL SUPPORT between 11 am & 11.45 p.m.	GR1
	24th	6 am 5 6 pm	3" Stokes fired intermittently throughout the day. 111 rounds being expended on enemy front system about O.8.d & O.8.b. On artillery were very active between 5.30 pm & 6.3 pm. Enemy artillery was active about 4.30 pm & 5.30 pm. Supports & Communication trenches being shelled (light barrage) Enemy shelled M5a.00.80 intermittently throughout day. The 12th French Mortar Battery was relieved by the 11th TMB3. relieved being complete by 6pm	GR1
ARRAS	24th	8 pm	Battery moved into billets.	GR1
	25th	9.30 am	Church Parade.	GR1
	26th	9 am 2 pm	Kit & Clothing inspection. Issue of clothing. Baths.	GR1
	27th	8-11.5am	Training in Albercourt Range. Reconstruct training. Personnel acted for instruction required Battalion. Three O.R. permanently attached	GR1

2449 Wt. W14957/M90 750,000 1/16 J.B.C. & A. Forms/C.2118/12.

Army Form C. 2118.

WAR DIARY
or
INTELLIGENCE SUMMARY.
(Erase heading not required.)

Instructions regarding War Diaries and Intelligence Summaries are contained in F. S. Regs., Part II. and the Staff Manual respectively. Title pages will be prepared in manuscript.

Place	Date Nov	Hour	Summary of Events and Information	Remarks and references to Appendices
ARRAS	28th	9 am	Close order drill, Gun drill, BF.	GRJ
		2 pm	Football (Recreational Training)	GRJ
	29th	9 am	Close order drill. Parade through Gas Chamber.	GRJ
	30th	9 am	Gun drill (rapid action) 11 am BF.	GRJ
		1.45 pm	Physical Training Instructor took class under Brigade Instruction.	

SECRET

WAR DIARY

OF

12TH T.M.B.

PERIOD

FROM: 1st DECEMBER 1917

TO: 31st DECEMBER 1917

Ashton. Captain
Commanding 12th Trench Mortar Btty.

2-1-18.

Army Form C. 2118.

WAR DIARY
or
INTELLIGENCE SUMMARY

(Erase heading not required.)

Instructions regarding War Diaries and Intelligence Summaries are contained in F. S. Regs., Part II. and the Staff Manual respectively. Title Pages will be prepared in manuscript.

Place	Date December	Hour	Summary of Events and Information	Remarks and references to Appendices
Field	1st		Bn in billets in ARRAS.	Reln
	2nd		Bn relieved 2" Seaforth Highlanders in Bde. Support in FOSSE FARM.	Reln
	3rd		Bn in Bde Reserve Support finding working parties.	Reln
	4th		" " " 1 O.R. Wounded	Reln
	5th		" " " 2 O.R. Killed, 1 O.R. wounded. 3 O.R. Reinforcements.	Reln
	6th		Bn relieved 1st K.O.R. Lanc. R. in front line Right Sub Sector, 1 O.R. Killed, 2 O.R. wounded	Reln
	7th		Bn in front line. 1 O.R. Wounded.	Reln
	8th		" " " 1 O.R. Wounded. 2 Lieut. W.F. HALL admitted to Hospl.	Reln
	9th		" " " Reinforcements 2 Lieut WILKINS & 97 O.R. Reinforcements 2 Lieut HEMSLEY.	Reln
	10th		Bn relieved by 1st K.O.R. Lanc. R. On relief moved into Bde. Reserve at Bois-des-Boeufs Camp.	Reln
	11th		Bn. in Bde. Reserve. Day and night working parties. Reinforcement 2 Lt. HERON.	Reln
	12th		Bn moved to Corps line 5.30 A.M.	Reln
	13th		Bn in Bde Reserve, Corps Line. 2 Lt. L.S. Adamson to Hospl.	Reln
	14th		Bn Relieved 1st K.O.R. Lanc. R in Right Sub Sector	Reln
	15th		Bn in front line. 1 O.R. Wounded.	Reln
	16th		" " " 1 O.R. "	Reln
	17th		" " " 1 O.R. " 4 O.R. Reinforcements.	Reln

Army Form C. 2118.

WAR DIARY
or
INTELLIGENCE SUMMARY
(Erase heading not required.)

Instructions regarding War Diaries and Intelligence Summaries are contained in F.S. Regs., Part II. and the Staff Manual respectively. Title Pages will be prepared in manuscript.

Place	Date December	Hour	Summary of Events and Information	Remarks and references to Appendices
Field	18th		Bn. relieved in trenches by 1st Som: L.I.	gen
ARRAS	19th		On relief Bn moved into Divl Reserve in ARRAS.	gen
"	20th		In Arras. Cleaning up.	gen
"	21st		" training. 8. O.R. Reinforcements	gen
"	22nd		" "	gen
"	23rd		" "	gen
"	24th		" " 2. O.R. Reinforcements	gen
"	25th		" "	gen
"	26th		Bn. moved up and relieved 3/10th Middlesex Regt. in MONCHY DEFENCES.	gen
Bde Support.	27th		Bde Support. Day slightly working parties	gen
"	28th		Bn in Bde Support. " " "	gen
"	29th		" " " " "	gen
"	30th		Bn relieved 1st K.O.R. Lanc R. in Right Sector, left sub sector	gen
"	31st		Bn in front line.	gen

4th Division
12d T. M. B.

January to April
1918

SECRET.

WAR DIARY.

OF

12TH T.M.B.

PERIOD.

FROM — 1st JANUARY 1918

TO — 31st JANUARY 1918

[signature] Captain
Commanding 12th. Trench Mortar Battery.

3rd. 2-18.

Army Form C. 2118.

WAR DIARY
or
INTELLIGENCE SUMMARY.
(Erase heading not required.)

Instructions regarding War Diaries and Intelligence Summaries are contained in F. S. Regs., Part II. and the Staff Manual respectively. Title pages will be prepared in manuscript.

Place	Date	Hour	Summary of Events and Information	Remarks and references to Appendices
NSd84	1/1/18	6 A.M.	Enemy attempted to fraternise at DEVIES TR. with men in front lines 3" Stokes fired 50 rounds and scattered them. 185 Rounds on enemy front and support lines. Total 8x Jacchie 185 Rounds	JW
		6 AM	20 rounds were fired on enemy trench in travels of gun (POOZE TR)	JW
	2/1/18	6 AM	100 rounds were fired on enemy front line DEVIES TR from BIT LANE to 6AM. I 32c 20-90 there were fired in bursts from 6PM to 4AM. 25 Rounds were fired a SPOON TR	JW
			& enemy retaliated with medium and light T.M.s & enemy sent up white lights into his front and supports. we shelled by 3" Stoken ground his dug in CURLY TR. 120 Rounds were fired in bursts of fire & enemy from there and	JW
	3/1/18	6 AM	supports during the period. Very little retaliation. enemy machine guns and snipers were silenced during the period.	JW
	4/1/18	6 AM	190 Rounds were fired during the period. Our S.O.S. went up in the left sector 3" Stokes opened out a S.O.S. lines 90 Rounds were fired. & enemy put down T.M. barrage on our front line	JW
		to	supports and communication trenches. Barrage came down at 10 P.M. and was over by 10-20 P.M. & enemy sent up following flares. Called for our artillery support. 6 orange light breaking into	JW
		6.	two. (Red descending into two Reds and W.S. Green lights). & Section upon 2W. Watch relieved No 2 Sector & W. fired	JW

A584. Wt. W4973/M687 750,000 8/16 D. D. & L. Ltd. Forms/C.2118/13.

Army Form C. 2118.

WAR DIARY
or
INTELLIGENCE SUMMARY.
(Erase heading not required.)

Instructions regarding War Diaries and Intelligence Summaries are contained in F. S. Regs., Part II. and the Staff Manual respectively. Title pages will be prepared in manuscript.

Place	Date	Hour	Summary of Events and Information	Remarks and references to Appendices
N5 d 8090	5/1/19	6 A.m.	3" Stokes fired 30 rounds in bursts of fire on enemy machine gun at I32c 50-30 which was reported active. Enemy M.G. was silenced. 20 Rounds were fired on B17 LANE and junction with DEVILS TR. at 2 A.M. Enemy retaliated slightly. 300 Round ammunition carrying	JM
"	6/1/18	6 A.M.	6 junction order no 9 received. 30 rounds were fired on machine gun reported active at I32c 25-30. 20 rounds were fired on enemy emplacement where men were observed digging. 25 Rounds were fired on enemy from ema	JM JM
"	7/1/18	8 A.M.	20 Rounds were fired on active enemy machine gun and silenced at I32c 30-60. 35 Rounds were fired on enemy front line DEVILS TR during the period. Enemy TM were fairly active in our and enemy artillery active during the period.	JM JM
"	8/1/19	6 A.m.	30 Rounds were fired on machine gun at I32c 40-15. the machine gun was silenced at 8P.M. and did not fire again during the night. 30 Rounds were fired on DEVILS TR during the night. 50 Rounds were fired on enemy shell hole reported to be occupied at I32a 10-40. 2 mng retaliated very heavily on TM was put out of action by direct hit. Enemy opened to 10 rd	JM JM
"		6		JM

Army Form C. 2118.

WAR DIARY
or
INTELLIGENCE SUMMARY.
(Erase heading not required.)

Instructions regarding War Diaries and Intelligence Summaries are contained in F. S. Regs., Part II. and the Staff Manual respectively. Title pages will be prepared in manuscript.

Place	Date	Hour	Summary of Events and Information	Remarks and references to Appendices
N5 d 20/9	9/11/17	6 A.m.	100 Rounds were fired on enemy front line and supports in trunks of fir trees from 8 P.M. to 4 A.M. Enemy retaliated at 10 p.m. was on the whole fairly quiet.	JW
"	10/11/17	6 A.m.	50 Rounds were fired on enemy lines supplemented by 10 rounds with light shell emitters. Enemy over active from machine gun.	OJYM
"	11/11/17		Relieved by the 118 J.M.B. Relief complete by 5.15 P.M.	JM
Anas	12/11/17	9 A.m.	Boot cleaning inspection	JM
		2 P.M.	Section officers Parade	OJM
"	13/11/17		Church Parade	JM
"	14/11/15	9 A.m.	Drill	JM
	"	9 P.m.	Rifle cleaning drill	JM
"	15/1/15	9 A.M.	Arms & equipment	JM
		2 P.m.	Lecture	OJM

Army Form C. 2118.

WAR DIARY
or
INTELLIGENCE SUMMARY.
(Erase heading not required.)

Instructions regarding War Diaries and Intelligence Summaries are contained in F. S. Regs., Part II. and the Staff Manual respectively. Title pages will be prepared in manuscript.

Place	Date	Hour	Summary of Events and Information	Remarks and references to Appendices
Chas	16/1/18	9 AM	Musketry order. Rifle exercises.	JSM
"	"	11 AM	Route march.	JSM
"	"	2 PM	Football.	JSM
"	17/1/18	9 AM	Drill order. Arms drill, & rapid loading	JSM
"	"	2 PM	Lecture	JSM
"	18/1/18	9 AM	Rifle cleaning & Bathing parade	JSM
"	19/1/18	11 AM	Bombing harassing fire for the time being by No 10 L.T.M.B. in bright return. Our first No 2 Section under 2nd Lieut. Setter brought 1 look over gun in the line. No. 1 Section remained at Battery HQ. N.806.7. Relief complete 5.15 PM. 15 rounds long fused during the night.	JSM
N 806.7	20/1/18		3" Stokes Mortars fired 35 rounds on an gunposition at O.6.D.30.30. 50 rounds harassing fire in relation to E T.M. every autillery firing active during the period	JSM

A5834 Wt. W4973/M687 750,000 8/16 D. D. & L. Ltd. Forms/C.2118/13.

WAR DIARY
or
INTELLIGENCE SUMMARY.

Army Form C. 2118.

(Erase heading not required.)

Place	Date	Hour	Summary of Events and Information	Remarks and references to Appendices
N+P6.7	24/1/18		3" Stokes fired 35 rounds during the night on 036.05.15 & 030.00.50 enemy T.M. very active during the night. Enemy aircraft fairly active between 7 AM & 11 AM.	JSW
"	25/1/18		2.5 rounds were fired by 3" Stokes T. Mortars on 0309.1 during the night. 50 rounds fired on enemy front line the morning of 036.05.10. 2.0. T.M fired active throughout the night	JSW
"	26/1/18		3" Stokes fired on enemy lingtohren at 0390.65 30 rounds fired. M. gun active in the night. Enemy flaying was active throughout morning. Enemy aircraft active	JSW
"	28/1/18		3" Stokes fired on 20. Mi Gun position on 014.60.10. 15 rounds expended.	JSW

Army Form C. 2118.

WAR DIARY
or
INTELLIGENCE SUMMARY.
(Erase heading not required.)

Instructions regarding War Diaries and Intelligence Summaries are contained in F. S. Regs., Part II. and the Staff Manual respectively. Title pages will be prepared in manuscript.

Place	Date	Hour	Summary of Events and Information	Remarks and references to Appendices
N8067	24/1/18		E. T. M. fairly active shelling our front system during the morning. One 2. of plan was our lines during 13 to 9.11 AM being replied by our stokes trench.	J.W.
	"	11 AM	3" Stokes fired 30 rounds of on enemy ch. g. trenches at intervals on E. T. M. positions at O2 D 9.20. 50 rounds being fired at intervals during nil. at O14 B 60.15.	J.W.
	25/1/18	9.40 PM	E. T. M. active shelling our support lines.	J.W.
	26/1/18		3" Stokes fired 30 rounds at intervals during the night on E. M. 95. at O &D 60.55 and O S S 58.080 Machine gun active. retaliated to enemy bombardment.	J.W.
		2 AM	Our heavy artillery retaliated. Enemy very active.	J.W.
"	27/1/18		3" Stokes fired 30 rounds on enemy support lines, but eighteen were opened very quick. Machine guns active during night.	J.W.

A5834 Wt.W.4973/M687 750,000 8/16 D.D.&L.Ltd. Forms/C.2118/13.

Army Form C. 2118

WAR DIARY
or
INTELLIGENCE SUMMARY.
(Erase heading not required.)

Instructions regarding War Diaries and Intelligence Summaries are contained in F.S. Regs., Part II. and the Staff Manual respectively. Title pages will be prepared in manuscript.

Place	Date	Hour	Summary of Events and Information	Remarks and references to Appendices
N.9 D.6.7	28/1/18		3" Stokes fired 8 rounds on enemy front system. Hostile artillery quiet. H.Sh. guns active during the night.	JAW
"	29/1/18		3" Stokes fired 30 on enemy front system. Enemy T.M. quiet.	JAW
			M.guns machine normal.	
"	30/1/18		3" Stokes fired 30 rounds on enemy support lines. Our M.G. active during the night. E.T.M's inactive	JAW
"	31/1/18		3" Stokes inactive. E. artillery quiet. E. T.M's fired 40 rounds on our front & support lines at 3.15 P.M. 12"Rle. 00s No 107 and 105 fired.	JAW

SECRET.

WAR DIARY

OF

12TH. T.M.B.

PERIOD FROM 1st. FEBRUARY 1918

TO 28TH. FEBRUARY 1918.

J.B.Shaw Captain
Commanding 12th. Trench Mortar Battery

3. 3. 18.

WAR DIARY or INTELLIGENCE SUMMARY

Army Form C. 2118.

Place	Date	Hour	Summary of Events and Information	Remarks and references to Appendices
N5 D 8.9.	1/2/18	6 AM	Ammunition expended 35 Rounds. 3" Stokes fired on enemy front system in retaliation to enemy T.M.s. 5 Rounds fired on enemy M.G. emplacements.	
"	2/2/18	6 AM	3" Stokes fired our fire system during the night with S.O.S guns. 3" Stokes put down a barrage for the 2/8 Batt. D of L of Wellington Regt. who raided the enemy front line with success.	
"	3/2/18	6 AM	3" Stokes fired 80 rounds during the period. 45 Rounds were fired on enemy front system. 35 Rounds were fired on O1.b.60.90 where an enemy M.G. had been reported	
"	4/2/18	6 AM	3" Stokes fired 50 rounds on enemy front system very quiet.	
"	5/2/18	6 "	12 " LMMs were relieved by the 1st X S.M.B. Relief completed at 7pm.	
"	6/2/18	6 "	The battery marched to ARRAS to billets for the night.	
"	7/2/18	6 "	1st X LMMs marched to rest billets at BERNEVILLE with the rest of the Brigade.	
BERNEVILLE	7/2/18	6 M	Battery paraded at 9 AM and 2 PM. The day was spent in cleaning up equipment &c.	
"	8/2/18		Parade 9 to 16 15" P.T. 10 to 11" cleaning of guns 1" to 1730 foot March.	
"	9/2/19		9 AM to 10 AM 10-30 to 11 LM Lift inspection 11 AM to 12-30 PM close order drill and rifle exercise drill.	
"	10/2/18		Church Parade C of E 10 AM Catholics 11 AM Nov. 10-30	

Army Form C. 2118.

WAR DIARY
or
INTELLIGENCE SUMMARY.
(Erase heading not required.)

Instructions regarding War Diaries and Intelligence Summaries are contained in F. S. Regs., Part II. and the Staff Manual respectively. Title pages will be prepared in manuscript.

Place	Date	Hour	Summary of Events and Information	Remarks and references to Appendices
BERNEVILLE	11/2/18		Parade 8-45 AM drill order 8-45 AM to 10-45 drill & PT. 11-0 to 12-30 gun drill. 2 pm to 3 pm NCO's class 5-6 Lecture	9 Oh.
"	12/2/18		Parade 8-45 AM drill order 8-45 AM to 10-45 Bayonet fighting + gun drill 11 to 12-30 pm Drill and musketry 2-3 pm NCO's class 5 pm 6 pm Lecture	9 Ch.
	13/2/18		Parade 8-45 fighting order 8-45 to 10-45 AM Route march 11 to 12-30 musketry and ceremonial drill. Half holiday sectional football match	9 Ch.
	14/2/18		Parade 8-45 fighting order 8-45 AM to 10-45 AM gun drill and bombing 11 AM to 12-30 PM deploying to attack 2 pm 2-30 pm Lecture 5-6 NCO's class	9 Ch.
	15/2/18		Parade 8-45 fighting order gun drill and PT from 9 am to 10-45. Tactical scheme defended gun positions 11 to 12-30 pm 2-3 NCO's class 5-6 Lecture 9-45 am to 9-45 am Cleaning billets 10 pm 12-30 pm Route march to Dainville	9 Ch.
	16/2/18		fighting order. Staff Holiday football match	9 Ch.
	17/2/18		Church Parade at 10 am C of E. 9-15 war: 10-45 R.C.	9 W.
	18/2/18		Parade 8.30 fighting order Rifle drill and PT 8-30 to 10-30 AM 10-45 am to 12-30 rapid digging in gun pits 2-3 pm NCO's class + Lecture 5-6 Lecture	9 Ct.
	19/2/18		Parade at 8-30 am fighting order marched to T.M. Range near Warley fired 30 rounds each track at 12-30 pm	9 W.
	20/2/18		Parade 8-30 fighting order Brigade scheme 2-3: Lecture on ammunition Half holiday	9 Ch.
	21/2/18		Parades fighting order 8-30 am to 12-30. 2-0 pm Lecture	9 Ct.
	22/2/18		Parades fighting order 8-30 am to 12-30 pm 2-0 Lecture	9 Ch.

WAR DIARY or INTELLIGENCE SUMMARY.

Army Form C. 2118.

Place	Date	Hour	Summary of Events and Information	Remarks and references to Appendices
BERNEVILLE	23/2/18		Parade at 8-30 pm fighting order football match	
	24/2/18		Church Parade C of E 9.10-45 am R.C. 10 a-	
	25/2/18		Parade at 8-45 fighting order 2-0 pm Lecture	gas
	26/2/18		Parade at 8-45 fighting order 2-0 pm Lecture	gas
	27/2/18		Parade 8-45 am to 12-30 pm fighting order 2-0 pm NCO's class 5 th & 6 th Lecture	gas
	28/2/18		Parade 8-45 am to 12-30 pm fighting order 2-0 pm NCO's class	gas

Army Form C. 2118.

WAR DIARY
or
INTELLIGENCE SUMMARY.
(Erase heading not required.)

Instructions regarding War Diaries and Intelligence Summaries are contained in F. S. Regs., Part II. and the Staff Manual respectively. Title pages will be prepared in manuscript.

Place	Date	Hour	Summary of Events and Information	Remarks and references to Appendices
BERNEVILLE	1/3/18		Parade fighting order 8.30 am - P.T. open drill 1.15.30 2.0pm lecture	
	2/3/18		Parade at 8.30 am - fighting order - P.T. Hurdles - 9-12.30 2.0pm Gas stunt	
	3/3/18		Parade at 8.30 am - Route march - Football match	
	4/3/18		Church Parade - Coff. 10 am Catholics Mass Menchecourt 10.30 am	
	5/3/18		Parade 8.30 am fighting order - P.T. - Gunns 9 - 10.30. Lecture 10.45-12.15 2.0pm Gun drill	
	6/3/18		Parade 8.30 am fighting order - Special Battn H.Q. 9 - 10 am Cleaning of 2.0pm	
	7/3/18		Parade 8.30 am - Inspection of fighting equipment 2.0pm Cleaning equipment	
	8/3/18		Parade 8.30 am Gun drill 9 - 10.30 PT Ropes 10.45 - 12.30 pm	
	9/3/18		Battery paraded at 9 am 2.0pm football match	
			Parade at 9.30 Kit Inspection followed 9.15-12.30pm - 2.0pm Brigade Path.	
	11/3/18		Battery parade at 9.0 am Lecture P.T./Gunn 9.15-12.30pm 2.0pm Football match	
	12/3/18		Church Parade. Coff. 10 am Catholics 11 am Hockey team 10.30 am	
	14/3/18		Parade at 8.30 am. Battery moved to Arras -	

Army Form C. 2118.

WAR DIARY
or
INTELLIGENCE SUMMARY.
(Erase heading not required.)

Instructions regarding War Diaries and Intelligence Summaries are contained in F. S. Regs., Part II. and the Staff Manual respectively. Title pages will be prepared in manuscript.

Place	Date	Hour	Summary of Events and Information	Remarks and references to Appendices
ARRAS	13/2/18		Parade 9.15 am. Inspection of Mens clothing etc. General cleaning general of battery	W.S.A
	14/2/18		Parade 9.15 am. Battery allowed at Gas school to test Gas Helmets 9-12.0 2 p.m. Route March	W.S.A
	15/2/18		Parade 9 am. Gun drill + P.T. 9.15 - 12.30 pm. 2 o pm Football match	W.S.A
	16/2/18		Parade 9 am. Gun drill - Gas drill + PT 9.15 - 12.30 pm - 2 pm Lecture on Construction of Battery	W.S.A
	17/2/18		Parade 9 am - Cleaning of guns etc - 2.0 pm. Voluntary	W.S.A
	18/2/18		Parade Church - C of E. 10 am. R.C. 11 am. Voluntary. 10.30 pm.	W.S.A
	19/2/18		Proceeded to Battery position in front line. 1st TMB relieved 2nd GUARDS TMB.	W.S.A
1.7 B-10-20	20/2/18	12.30 am 6 pm	3" T.M. inaction	W.S.A W.S.A
	20/2/18	6 am	3" Mortars fired 123 rounds between 9.15 pm + 5 am on Enemy front lines in retaliation	W.S.A
	21/2/18	6 am	3" Mortars fired 35 rounds on enemy front line at 7.15 pm	W.S.A
	22/2/18	6 am	3" L.T.M. Mortars fired 35 rounds - 7.45 - 8.15 pm + 20 rounds at 9.0 pm on Enemy front line	W.S.A

WAR DIARY
or
INTELLIGENCE SUMMARY.

Army Form C. 2118.

Instructions regarding War Diaries and Intelligence Summaries are contained in F. S. Regs., Part II. and the Staff Manual respectively. Title pages will be prepared in manuscript.

(Erase heading not required.)

Place	Date	Hour	Summary of Events and Information	Remarks and references to Appendices
17 B.10.20	23/8/18	6 am	3" T.M. inaction. enemy	W.g.A
	24 "	6 am	3" Mortars fired 80 rounds on front line between 6.30 am & 5.45 am	G.g.A
	25 "	6 am	3" L.T.M. fired 40 rounds between 7.45 pm & 9 pm on enemy M.G.	W.g.A
	26 "	6 am	3" " fired 115 rounds on enemy front line at 7.30 pm & 9 pm	W.g.A
	27-30- 3-1-18		German Offensive Start. Fired 800 rounds - 6 guns put out of action - 1 officer & 10 other ranks casualties.	W.g.A
	31-3-18	6 am	3" L.T.M. fired 10 rounds during night on M.G. & 11 B.60 & 20 rounds on trench junction	W.g.A

Johnson Lieut.
O.C. 12" TMB

12th Brigade.

4th Division.

12th LIGHT TRENCH MORTAR BATTERY

APRIL 1918.

SECRET

WAR DIARY
of
12th TRENCH MORTAR BATTERY

PERIOD 1st APRIL 1918
to
30th APRIL 1918.

M. Irwin Capt.
O/C 12 Trench Mortar Battery.

1.5.18

Army Form C. 2118.

WAR DIARY
or
INTELLIGENCE SUMMARY.
(Erase heading not required.)

Instructions regarding War Diaries and Intelligence Summaries are contained in F. S. Regs., Part II. and the Staff Manual respectively. Title pages will be prepared in manuscript.

Place	Date	Hour	Summary of Events and Information	Remarks and references to Appendices
F/B 10-20	1/4/18	6 Am	3" Stokes Mortars fired 40 rounds on enemy working parties in HARP TR. Several shots were observed and alarmed and lowering parties of the enemy scattered. Hostile shelling heavy.	Jal.
	2/4/18	6 Am	3" Stokes Mortar fired 20 rounds during the night on enemy trenches with good effect. Hostile artillery still fairly active	Jal.
	3/4/18	6 Am	Enemy raided trenches at 6-30 Am fairly about 200 strong. 3" Stokes of ours fired caught enemy in no mans land inflicting heavy casualties. 2nd Lieut W.S. De Jarnus relieved 2nd Lt J.G. Herman in front line.	Jal.
	4/4/18	6 Am	3" Stokes did not fire. Enemy artillery quiet. Our artillery active.	Jal.
	5/4/18	6 Am	3" Stokes fired 90 Rounds on enemy trenches and working parts. Several direct hits were obtained.	Jal.
	6/4/18	6 Am	3" Stokes fired 20 rounds on enemy machine guns. Hostile artillery active during the night. Our support trenches. Our artillery retaliated on enemy trenches.	W.
	7/4/18	6 Am	12" French Mortar Battery relieved by Canadian trench mortar Battery relief completed by 11 pm. 12 TMB's proceeded to billets in SIMON COURT. hq right railway.	Jal.

WAR DIARY
or
INTELLIGENCE SUMMARY

Army Form C. 2118.

Place	Date	Hour	Summary of Events and Information	Remarks and references to Appendices
SIMONCOURT	8/4/18	6 am	The day was spent by unit cleaning equipment and clothing.	
"	9/4/18		Parade at 9 am. Kit, equipment etc. 10 am Clothing Inspection. Unit provided to bathe in the afternoon	
"	10/4/18		Parade at 9 am Rifle Inspection. Battalion inspected by G.O.C. Brigade.	
"	11/4/18	6 pm	The unit received orders to move with the rest of the Brigade to LILLERS. 12th GMB marched to ARRAS-DOULLENS ROAD and	
"		6 am	entrained and proceeded to LILLERS. Arrived at LILLERS 9 pm. Billeted for the night at BUSNES.	
BUSNES	12/4/18	6 pm	9 pm unit still standing by, awaiting movement orders. No parade until movement orders received. Moved to L'ECLEME by route march	
L'ECLEME	13/4/18	6 am	Billeted in farms vacated by French people. Rifle Inspection and gun drill	
"	14/4/18	6 am	Rifle Inspection and P.T. Guns cleaned	
"	15/4/18	6 am	Route march in fighting order. No parade in afternoon	

WAR DIARY
or
INTELLIGENCE SUMMARY.
(Erase heading not required.)

Army Form C. 2118.

Place	Date	Hour	Summary of Events and Information	Remarks and references to Appendices
	16/4/18	6 p.m	No parades. 12th J.M.B relieved 11th J.M.B at GONNEHAM	gm.
	17/4/18	6 p.m	11th J.M.B had not been in action.	
		6 p.m	2 Trench Mortars under 2nd Lieut L.J. Horman go into action at RIEZ DU VINAGE	gm.
	18/4/18	6 p.m	Ammunition expended nil. Heavy hostile bombardment	gm.
	19/4/18	6 p.m	from 130 rounds were fired at dawn after heavy barrage dashing from Enemy artillery active. No enemy attack developed	gm.
	20/4/18		Acting 2nd Lieut W Harrold relieves 2nd Lt L.J. Horman on the line. No trench mortar action.	gm.
	21/4/18	6 p.m	Artillery active on both sides. Ammunition expended by Stokes nil.	gm.
	22/4/18	6 a.m	11th Brigade attacked at 5.15 am to capture portion of PACAUT WOOD objective and 53rd Stokes assisted in barrage. 146 rounds were fired.	gm.
	23/4/18	6 p.m	2nd Batt Lan Fus captured few houses and prisoners 3rd Stokes fired 621 Rounds	gm.

Army Form C. 2118.

WAR DIARY
or
INTELLIGENCE SUMMARY.
(Erase heading not required.)

Maps on France 36a 1/40000

Place	Date April	Hour	Summary of Events and Information	Remarks and references to Appendices
LÉCLUSE	14th		Batty. relieved by 107TH Bde/Gng in ROEUX sector our personnel & material left	
	25th		LÉCLUSE	
	26th		Uneventful day. Little enemy counterfire and scarce hostile aircraft	
	27th			
U Bde RFA	28th		Battery relieved 117TH Batty in Rœux sector less two. Prompt & efficient Recce.	
			Shelling of roads and CANAL BANKS. Slight casualties during relief. Two guns	
			active in present lines.	
	29th		Quiet day generally. TM's machine and artillery fire	
	30th		Our artillery active. TM's fast in enemy positions in wood Counter-prep. held	
			enemy attack opposite our available front.	

www.ingramcontent.com/pod-product-compliance
Lightning Source LLC
Chambersburg PA
CBHW081440160426
43193CB00013B/2337